mad girl

Also by Bryony Gordon:
The Wrong Knickers: A Decade of Chaos

mad girl

BRYONY GORDON

headline

First published in 2016
by HEADLINE PUBLISHING GROUP

1

Cataloguing in Publication Data is available from the British Library

Hardback ISBN 978 1 4722 3208 3
Trade Paperback ISBN 978 1 4722 3670 8

Typeset in Berling by Palimpsest Book Production Ltd, Falkirk, Stirlingshire

Printed and bound in Great Britain by Clays Ltd, St Ives plc

Headline's policy is to use papers that are natural, renewable and recyclable
products and made from wood grown in sustainable forests. The logging and
manufacturing processes are expected to conform to the environmental
regulations of the country of origin.

HEADLINE PUBLISHING GROUP
An Hachette UK Company
Carmelite House
50 Victoria Embankment
London EC4Y 0DZ

www.headline.co.uk
www.hachette.co.uk

For the one in four. The We

'I think I made you up inside my head'
Sylvia Plath
Mad Girl's Love Song

Contents

Prologue

I need to be honest with you from the start – because, as you will see, this is an honest book. A self-indulgent, self-flagellating, self-loathing book (at times, reading it back, I have wanted to shake myself), but an honest one, all the same. At times, maybe a little too honest. I have that problem sometimes. For instance, the other day, I was telling my best friend and her boyfriend all about the time my husband and I were having sex and my Fitbit started vibrating to tell me I had reached my daily exercise goal, which sent my other half into hysterics and put a halt to proceedings right then and there. My friend, she sort of smiled. Her boyfriend looked at his shoes. Me? I couldn't work out why they weren't both rolling around on the floor laughing maniacally at this story that involved vibrating fitness trackers and my husband and I actually managing to have sex. I mean, what is wrong with these people?

In the spirit of honesty, I need to tell you right now that this is not a self-help book. If you are looking for that, you have really come to the wrong place. I have absolutely no qualifications to write one. In fact, I barely have any qualifications at all, bar a few GCSEs, a tiny-titted handful of A-levels and some swimming badges from childhood. It would be simply preposterous for me to pretend that this is some kind of self-help book when, as the next 300 or so pages will show you, I have spent most of my life not being able to help myself when it comes to food and drugs and booze, and have only relatively recently even thought about a solid course of therapy or a gym membership.

No miracle cure for mental illness is to be found in this book. I cannot say that reading it will change your life or transform your wellbeing or any of the other frankly wild claims made by so many of the millions of self-help books out there on the market. Please don't cry. I hope that in saying this I have not made you feel too bleak or despairing (I am guessing that, in picking up this book, these are things you might be going through – or things you have in the past gone through and are keen to avoid going through again in the future). What I mean is I'm not a doctor, or a qualified expert in mental illness. But I have had a lot of experience of it. I've been dogged by it my entire adult life. I know what it feels like.

And yet, despite my tendency towards over-sharing, I have not always been honest about the stuff that has gone on in my head. Some of you reading this may have also read my first book, *The Wrong Knickers*, which was a somewhat candid document of my crazy twenties. In it, I wrote about the time a man tried to use Lurpak as a sexual lubricant. I wrote about hooking up with someone in a sexual health clinic. I wrote about catching nits from a barman and having an affair with a married man and flashing my boobs in a pub. But despite all of this excessive honesty, I did not write about my periods of depression, my battle with obsessive compulsive disorder (OCD), or my years with bulimia. I did not write about these things because – even as recently as 2013, when I was writing *The Wrong Knickers* – I couldn't. I was too ashamed, too frightened, too convinced I was a freak to admit to any of the things that had cluttered up my head for so long. I would literally rather write about a man snorting cocaine off my breasts than I would about my mental health (although it was probably clear to readers of *The Wrong Knickers* that I wasn't always entirely of sane mind). I made out that the first and only time I went on antidepressants was when I had a breakdown on my thirtieth birthday, because how could I admit, casually, that I had actually been on them since I was seventeen? I made out that I had lost a tooth because of excessive sugar consumption, because how could I admit that it was actually because I had an eating disorder? Nor did I admit to having been in an abusive relationship. I didn't want anyone to think that I was an emotional wreck or a drama queen. Because that's what we always call a woman who has 'issues', don't we? A drama queen. An attention seeker.

Then, a few months after the book came out in 2014, I experienced a serious episode of OCD. I couldn't do anything except cry and ruminate and have panic attacks. I had a breakdown, basically, my fifth in twenty years, and I'd had enough – I'd had enough of the secrecy and the silence and all the fearful lying that I was fine, that we were all of us always fucking fine when one in four of us will at some point absolutely *not* be fine, one in four being the number of people who experience mental-health problems. And if that's the case, then four in four of us probably know someone who suffers. 'How are you?' people always politely ask when bumping into someone, and 'I'm fine' is always, always the answer, even when it's a barefaced lie.

So I decided I was not going to collude with this lie any more. I decided I was going to tell the truth – and to hell if people thought I was weird, or a drama queen, or an attention seeker. If, as a journalist who writes personal columns and candid books, *I* felt I couldn't admit to these things, then what hope was there for everyone else? What hope did we have in destroying the stigma attached to mental illness? Perhaps this sudden change of heart came about because I was now a mother, and didn't want my own child to live in a world where the mentally ill are forced to exist as if everything was tickety-fucking-boo. Perhaps it was brilliant people including Ruby Wax and Matt Haig talking about their own experiences of depression. Whatever it was, when I sat down to write my column in the *Telegraph* that bleak week in January 2014, I resolved finally to be really, properly honest about myself.

'I begin the new year by falling into a deep depression,' I wrote. 'I don't mean this in a jokey way. It really does happen. If I'm honest, it's been going on a while, but you can't write that in a column over the festive period. "Happy Christmas! And by the way, I'm really depressed." So I've ignored it and ignored it and ignored it for as long as I could, but as anyone who has suffered from the black dog will know, the black dog will not be ignored forever.'

And then later, when writing about going to see the GP about it: 'The doctor's waiting room is cold and the walls are a disconcerting shade of orange, like nicotine. There are people coughing and sneezing while some just stare into the middle distance, and I wonder if they are like me, or if I am like them. I wonder if they too have the disease whose only outward symptom is a jaw clamped shut through tension, or frantic tapping on any available surface. Diseases of the mind. What I would do right now for a cough or a cold or even a broken leg. Anything but this. (Oh God, depression is so self-indulgent.)'

The day the first column was published, my inbox witnessed what you might term a deluge of emails. Of all the subjects I had written about in my career, not one of them had elicited a response like this, and not a single person trolled me or told me that nobody cared. Over the next few weeks I received hundreds and hundreds of messages from people sharing their own stories of mental illness. Strangers sent me cards. Friends I had always seen as upbeat and jolly, who had probably always seen me as upbeat and jolly, pulled me to one side and told me about the diseases in their own minds. And I had a lightbulb moment, a moment of complete clarity, when I realised that, far from being weird, mental illness was absolutely *normal*.

So many of us experience it, and yet so few of us feel able to talk about it, and despite promises by politicians to take mental health as seriously as physical health, it is clear that this is simply not the case. As this book was being put to bed, an independent commission supported by the Royal College of Psychiatrists and headed by a former NHS chief executive found that a lack of funding to mental-health services in England was putting some of society's most vulnerable people at risk. Severely ill people are routinely being sent hundreds of miles away from home for care due to a lack of available beds – something, the report's authors pointed out, that would never happen to people suffering a heart attack or a stroke. Campaigners often use the broken-arm analogy when trying to fight for parity between mental and physical health services – why should a broken brain be treated any less seriously? – but the sad truth is that unless you have experienced a broken brain yourself, it is very difficult to understand the urgent need for better care.

Then there was the mental-health audit that came out the very day I finished this book, which found that mental illness is the largest single cause of disability in this country, suicides are on the rise, and sufferers have been let down by a governance system that is in many ways fuelling the epidemic. The NHS report called on David Cameron to invest £1 billion in a comprehensive shake-up of mental-health provision and warned that, as things stand, the NHS is to blame for about 400 suicides a year.

Four hundred people. Every year.

That is simply not acceptable.

According to the charity Rethink Mental Illness, budgets for mental-health trusts were cut by 8.25 per cent during the last parliament, despite referrals to community mental-health teams rising by nearly 20 per cent in the same time. Only 5.5 per cent of the UK health research budget is given to mental health, despite poor mental health carrying an economic and social cost of £105 billion a year in England alone. A happy country is a healthy country, and yet pluck up the courage to go to a doctor and ask for help and you'll be lucky if you get it before the next giant asteroid is due to hit planet Earth in 20 million years. I'm making this up. It's not an official statistic, just so you know – that asteroid could hit in 65 million years or next week for all the knowledge I have of space. But the point is, mental-health provisions in this country are so piss poor that entire seasons have come and gone while people have waited to see a professional therapist on the NHS. Babies have been born, *Game of Thrones* books have been written, glaciers have melted.

While writing this book, I read about the Briton who lay down over his girlfriend to protect her as all around them ISIS gunmen shot dead innocent Parisian concert goers. When he went to his doctor and asked if he could see a counsellor to talk about what had happened, he was told he first had to go through a three-month 'watchful waiting' time. Then there was the young mother who committed suicide on the same day as calling a mental-health clinic to tell them she was too unwell to make an appointment. NHS rules meant that the worker she spoke to could not ask any questions about her health. The young mother was later discharged from the service for not attending another appointment. Absolutely no effort had been made to check on her welfare – had anyone bothered to do this they would have discovered that the reason for her non-attendance was because she was dead. At her inquest, the coroner described the system as 'bonkers': 'I shouldn't have to use words like bonkers but I feel it's appropriate here.'

Each and every week, the papers report on another failure in mental-health care – the ill adults and *children* held in police cells because of a shortage of space in NHS facilities; the problem of male suicide rates; the endless debate over the efficacy and dangers of antidepressants, and whether or not they are over-prescribed. Then again, what else are GPs supposed to do when presented with waiting lists and bed shortages that massive? Tell patients to get over themselves until a therapist becomes available? Send them on their way feeling even bleaker than when they went in?

Here's another frankly depresing story that came out while writing this book. Bootham Park, a mental hospital in York, closed suddenly because it was deemed unsafe for its patients. In 2014, a woman was found hanged in her room at the hospital. The Leeds and York Partnership NHS Foundation Trust admitted that a ligature point she used should have been removed. But alterations were a problem, as the hospital is Grade

I listed. This is by no means unusual. Ligature points are always being identified at mental-health units. Essentially what this shows us is that we live in a society that seems to value buildings over actual human beings.

Bootham Park started life in 1772 as the 'County Lunatic Asylum, York'. Its name may have changed over the years, but the infrastructure didn't. And while it seems we have come a long way since the days of the mentally ill being lobotomised, or routinely put through electroconvulsive therapy, the truth is that there is still a great way to go. The treatment of mental illness in this country is one of the great scandals of our time, and I hope that one day soon it will be widely recognised as such.

Only by talking about our own mental health will we start to be taken seriously. We need to shout about it; we need to tell as many people as possible about what goes on in our heads. So no, this is not a self-help book. It is just my story. My only hope is that by reading it, you might feel able to share yours, too.

1

I think I might be dying

It came to me in a dream. I know that sounds abso-lutely ridiculous, but it did, I promise you. One moment I was a regular twelve-year-old, working out which one of Take That I would marry,* praying that I would make it on to the netball A team because the B team would mean another year in social Siberia with my monobrow and the tartan socks my mother insisted I wore to school; the next, I was convinced I was dying of AIDS.

You know. All that normal pre-pubescent girl stuff.

I had gone to bed that Sunday night in December 1992 with only a passing knowledge of Acquired

---

* Preferred order: Robbie, Mark, Howard, Jason, Gary. I know this is controversial and that the list would eventually reverse itself, but bear with me, I was young.

Immune Deficiency Syndrome, gleaned almost entirely from an 'advert' warning of the dangers of unprotected sex and needle-sharing and umpteen other things that really shouldn't have bothered a twelve-year-old girl living in a terraced house with an Aga on the outer reaches of west London. I could go entire months without speaking to a boy and it would be years before I was even kissed by one. Recreational drugs were still at least a decade away and even then they never got intravenous. Indeed, on paper, I had absolutely nothing to worry about other than accidentally-on-purpose waking up my baby brother by stomping up the stairs in a huff. I had an annoying little sister who told everyone I farted into glasses, but, goodness, didn't everyone? Life was good – by any standard, life was great – and there was little to keep me awake at night as I snoozed in my bedroom, decorated with Designers Guild wallpaper that I had plastered over with posters of Take That, much to the horror of my mother. (This was a long time before the phrase 'first-world problems' existed, which is a shame, because I would have loved to throw it back at her every time she complained about a border being buggered up by Blu-Tack.)

To give you an idea of just how privileged I was, I should tell you that that afternoon I had actually attended the Smash Hits Poll Winners Party, which felt to me like the Oscars, if the Oscars were hosted by Simon Mayo and the goodie bags included flashing deely-boppers and bright pink whistles. It was the kind of thing most young girls would have given their right eye to go to at the time – most except the ones at my posh, all-girls school (you see? Such privilege) who saw pop music as totally lame and shallow and thought it was way cooler to be into Nirvana, because this showed you existed on a higher plane of consciousness or loftiness or whatever. (I should say that when Take That re-formed in the twenty-first century, and adulthood made it acceptable to admit to liking them, many of these girls – now grown women who should really have known better – claimed that they had *always* loved Take That, which I would have found deeply unjust if I hadn't had better things to do with my time, like shovelling cocaine up my nostrils or drinking my body weight in strong continental lager.)

Anyway, I had gone with my primary-school friend Emily, whose father happened to be in the music industry (yet more privilege), and we must have been the picture of innocence. I imagine us in floral dresses and T-bar shoes, because I am nostalgic like that, although in reality it was probably hideous Global Hypercolor T-shirts that blushed pink at the armpits, teamed with leggings and LA Lights trainers – the kind of thing that Hoxton hipsters wear now because they mistakenly believe that wearing things ironically will make them interesting (in much the same way my school friends thought liking Nirvana did). The Smash

Hits Poll Winners Party had been a spectacular event for Emily and me, less so for her dad, who spent the whole event with his hands over his ears, looking like a light had gone out behind his eyes. Take That cleaned up, walking away with such accolades as Best Group in the Whole Wide World, Most Fanciable Male, and Best Haircut (Mark, not Robbie, sadly, but still a win all the same). I now see that this must have been deeply demeaning to Mark, his vast musical talents reduced to the follicles on his pretty head, but at the time it made me feel joyous. It was vindication for choosing Take That. Was Kurt Cobain ever going to win best haircut? No! Was Dave Grohl ever going to saunter off with the most fanciable male title? I somehow doubted it.

We skipped out of Kensington Olympia on a high even though it was pouring with rain, and in the car back home we sang 'Could It Be Magic' over and over, telling Emily's dad to be quiet every time a new song came on the radio in case it was a Take That one. This was despite the fact that Emily's dad hadn't said anything for nearly two hours, and may have actually been in a catatonic state. I remember getting home and feeling a strange mixture of excitement and embarrassment as I described to my mum how totally amazing Take That were. I remember getting into bed with the sound of my own screams of delight ringing in my ears. I remember drifting off knowing that I had seen the man I was going to marry (Robbie) and that everything was going to be OK, netball A team or no netball A team. And this is the last time I remember life without darkness in my brain.

When I look back on my life and the mental illness that has defined so much of it, there is pre-dream Bryony, in her imaginary T-bars and Laura Ashley skirts, and there is post-dream Bryony, in Doc Martens and a perpetual frown. People often talk suspiciously of overnight transformations, but this really was one – I went to bed happy and woke up eight and a bit hours later in a state of turmoil, as if I had been abducted by aliens before being returned to my bed with a chip in my head. And who's to say this didn't happen? I mean, isn't it far more plausible than being sent nutso by a series of involuntary images and ideas that flash into your mind while you are unconscious? No. Don't answer that. Already I am worried that you think I am bonkers.

Anyway, I know that listening to other people's dreams is only marginally less tedious than transcribing minutes from a meeting about treatment for fungal infections, so I will keep this brief. This may seem like selflessness, but in actual fact my linguistic parsimony is because the dream was as dull as dishwater. It wasn't particularly vivid or detailed. I remember very little of it, other than that it was the start of a long civil war in my head, the effects of which would every now and then be felt in other parts of my body, as if refugees had fled my brain and sought solace elsewhere – in a gaunt cheekbone, for example, or a pronounced clavicle. Basically, I dreamt that I had an incurable disease. I didn't look ill, or feel ill. I was up and doing all the things I usually did, including going to school, playing Nintendo and watching *The Simpsons*. But in my dream a doctor told me I was dying and that was that. No respite. I would be dead in months. Days, maybe.

I remember a friend at a sleepover telling us all, in a terribly serious tone, that if you die in a dream, you die in real life. Perhaps that was why I woke up in a cliché of cold sweat, convinced that it was all over, my nightmare not a fevered dream caused by watching an advert but a terrible premonition of things to come. I had read in a newspaper that people with HIV didn't know they had it until it was too late and the virus had developed into AIDS. Perhaps this explained why in my dream I had been given a death sentence while outwardly appearing well. Yes, that was it – it made perfect sense. I was dying of AIDS, and I wasn't even a teenager yet.

I honestly thought I would never become a teenager.

Although I don't remember too much detail of the dream, the weeks afterwards have all the nightmarish detail of a Salvador Dali painting. At school that day everyone chatted excitedly about their weekends and

I remember feeling a great weight above my heart because I thought that I would never again be able to do the same. All the joy I had felt after the Smash Hits Poll Winners Party had evaporated. I could scarcely believe that the girl tunelessly singing 'Could It Be Magic' the day before was me. During maths I almost wept for the mundane anxiety I used to feel when I couldn't do quadratic equations. In English I wondered why I had ever panicked about the late handing in of an essay about Shakespeare. These seemed to me such simple worries and I would have given anything for them that first winter of discontent. As it was, all I could think about was how I had managed to catch AIDS, or how I was almost certainly about to catch AIDS, from a splinter in my desk or a rogue needle I hadn't seen on the tube.

Everywhere I looked, I saw danger. Germs lurked on every surface, even if they weren't visible. In fact, if they weren't visible, didn't that make them more dangerous? I was terrified of the seventies-style seats on the tube, not because they were an eyesore but because they had an orangey hue that I felt could disguise blood stains. In time, I stopped sitting down unless I absolutely had to. It was easier than checking a seat ten, fifteen, twenty times. When the Christmas holidays finally turned up, I simply stopped going out at all.

But I am getting ahead of myself a bit. I developed other idiosyncrasies, too, although the word idiosyncrasy implies they were funny little habits that I had affected in order to provide myself with some depth, like a love of Nirvana, for example. But I would really rather not have had to leave the room every time a Queen song came on (a year before, Freddie Mercury had died of AIDS) so that I could chant the name of Freddie Starr over and over again, Starr being a 'healthy' Freddie who would counteract the presence of the 'unhealthy' Freddie. I would really rather not have spent hours in the library, reading about lesions and oral thrush and all the other symptoms of AIDS that young girls needn't learn about, so that I could spot the signs when I eventually developed them. And I would really rather not have then had to run home to scrub my body and wash my hair and throw away my clothes just in case anything nasty had been transferred from the books.

There was no logic to what was going on in my head – a rhyme, maybe, a never-ending death song, but absolutely no reason. My encyclopedic knowledge should have eventually empowered me and reassured me that, actually, everything was fine – unlike many other people in the early nineties, I knew you could not catch HIV from toilet seats or shared cups – but instead it made everything worse. It fed my anxiety instead of starving it. My imagination found ever more alarming ways for danger to strike. I could accidentally step on a discarded hypodermic needle in the park.

I could have been infected by the surgeon who removed my appendix in 1989. I could be in a café and someone could sneeze and the sneeze could contain tiny globules of blood that could land on my eyeballs without me even knowing, your eyeballs being one of the most permeable parts of your body. And who was to say that the disease wouldn't evolve and become airborne? Scientists, probably, but I wasn't one of them and I didn't know any and so off my imagination went, coming up with more and more elaborate ways for me to die before I had reached my thirteenth birthday.

I was so scared of blood on my hands that I began to wash them as often as possible, the irony being that they soon started to crack and bleed. Some people's hands are covered in liver spots; mine were covered in blood spots. I was Lady Macbeth, without the murderous impulses (I hoped). At night I lay in bed staring hard at the scabs on my red raw hands, checking to see if they had turned green. Green, I had decided in my not very logical way, was a sign of infection. If they were still red, then perhaps everything was fine. I wore gloves as much as I could but this in itself was not without danger, because who knew who had handled them while they were still on sale in the shop? Clothes with pockets posed a similar problem, but in a rare moment of lucidity I reasoned that they were better than nothing.

19

I would have worn bandages round my hands if I could have.

Christmas was coming and joy was everywhere but I couldn't share in it. I helped to decorate the tree in the solemn belief that it was probably the last time I would ever do so. The smiling carol singers and the laughing Father Christmasses on the television seemed to make my misery more acute. Everyone's happiness seemed obscene given what was going on in my head. I simply could not comprehend how normal life could continue when I felt so abnormal.

I had started to hide my toothbrush under my pillow instead of keeping it in the bathroom because I was terrified I would pass my illness to my family. I stopped holding my baby brother, or playing with my annoying little sister, because as annoying as she was I did not want her to die. It was one thing living with the possibility of being ill yourself, quite another with the possibility you might have condemned someone you love to the same fate.

You may be wondering what my parents made of this behaviour, but I am not sure that they even noticed. It was winter, so of course my hands were chapped. I was almost a teenager, so of course I didn't want to share bathroom things with them or see my friends when school broke up. Of course I wanted to stay in my room staring sullenly at Blu-Tacked borders. Adolescence was approaching, fast, and nothing about my moodiness and separateness was really that strange. This too will pass, I imagine they said after hearing yet another slammed door.

On Christmas Eve, my mum suggested we go out and buy some last-minute presents. I remember her trying to take my hand only for me to stuff it in my pocket in terror. She must have thought I was embarrassed by the gesture, her little girl all grown up, when in actual fact I longed to clasp her fingers in mine, to feel the warmth in them and the love. But I was too scared of my blood infecting her, too convinced that I was actually poisonous. A couple of days later she would spin me round the kitchen to the Pogues' 'Fairytale of New York' and for a moment I would laugh uproariously and remember what it was like before I became certain I was dying, but then the reality of my situation snapped back in and I spent the next week convinced this one, tiny gesture had condemned my mother to death.

That Christmas Eve, when she managed to get me out of the house, we went to Woolworths and Our Price and the toy shop on the corner and then finally we went to Boots, to stock up on nappies for my eight-month-old brother, whom I was tasked with looking after in his pram while my mother paid at the counter. But I couldn't do it, not even for thirty seconds. I knew I couldn't protect him from the germs, or the diseased people picking up their prescriptions from the pharmacy. What if one of them tried to hold him, or ruffle his hair? For a moment I stopped breathing. I was certain that my heart was trying to escape from my chest. It wanted to burst through my ribcage and out on to the floor of the shop where it would inevitably become infected with some hideous disease. I pushed the pram out while hyperventilating and crying, the people around me presumably trying to work out whether or not to call the police about a potential child abduction. Later that afternoon, having dropped my brother back at home so he could be under the watchful eye of my father and nine-year-old sister, Mum took me to the Christmas fair to try to calm me down. We went on the bumper cars, and for the four and a half minutes we were on them all my worries were suspended, forgotten about, left on the side with the people waiting their go. I counted the minutes on the Flik Flak watch I'd got for my birthday six months before, when everything was normal and fine and happy and I had my whole life ahead of me. I counted those four and a half minutes under my breath, and I wanted them never to end.

I know what you must be thinking. You must be thinking: where on earth did *that* come from? Was it a manifestation of some abuse I had been suffering from secretly? Nope. None of that. Was it the result of bullying at school, caused by a tricky combination of my monobrow and love of Take That? No. Not that either – I was so utterly mediocre that people barely noticed me, let alone bullied me. Had I had an unhappy childhood, filled with bile and recriminations? Hardly. I lived in a house with an Aga and a cat called Moppet, and the family car was a Volvo.

I suppose, looking back, I was a somewhat anxious child. My stocking was left outside the front door as I thought it unwise to allow a strange man into the house, even if he did come laden down with presents. Surely Father Christmas was the ultimate stranger bearing sweets? I was worried about fire so I kept a small red bell by my bed that would enable me to alert the rest of my family should there be a blazing inferno. When I realised that I might be overcome by the smoke first, I insisted on small red bells for everyone.

As a toddler, I was convinced that there was a monster in the sky every time a storm blew up, and one of my earliest memories is huddling behind the sofa with my mother, hiding from someone I thought was a murderous intruder, although she tells me it would more likely have been a nosy neighbour she didn't want to see. At six, I developed a fear of nuclear war – you know, monsters under the bed, sleeping in the dark, atom bombs obliterating you in seconds, that kind of thing – and at seven it became of great concern to me that we might have to live at the top of a very high tree. I'd seen a news report about the likelihood of London flooding in the year 2005 due to the Thames Barrier failing because of some catastrophic weather event. This was 1987, so 2005 was a very long way off, but that didn't stop me from worrying about the logistics of living in said very high tree. Would we have to swim everywhere? Develop gills? Build a boat?

Acid rain was a real worry, as was the hole in the ozone layer. You never hear about these things any more, but in the eighties they were all anyone ever banged on about, an environmental ISIS ready to pounce and destroy at any moment. When I read columns concerned about a generation of children growing up under the scourge of social media and the internet, I think, 'Spare me! These kids have NO idea how good they've got it. You think we had it easier, worrying that our skin was going to burn off and melt away every time it rained, which was often, by the way? You think not having Facebook and Snapchat makes up for the fact that every time we left the house, the sun's deadly rays could have killed us instantaneously? Man up, children of the twenty-first century! Man up!' Mad cow disease was a ticking time bomb that lurked in all of our bodies. And as for CFCs, which were lethal and poisonous and in *everything*, just so you know . . . well, simply putting your deodorant on in the morning had the power to destroy the planet.

My mother bought me a set of Mexican worry dolls to keep under my pillow because in my mind lurked a whole host of things I was certain were going to go bump in the night – Gremlins, the goblins from *Labyrinth*, Freddy Kreuger, Chucky. Video nasties threatened the very fabric of society. Lights were always left on at bedtime, but daybreak was no guarantee of safety. Public information films, shown to you at school, and then repeated on telly just in case you weren't traumatised enough, showed children with limbs amputated or being burnt alive after chasing footballs on to train lines or in to electricity pylons.

It was a worrying time to be a child, but then I imagine it is always a worrying time to be a child. And none of these things were, in themselves, reasons for me to have spent two weeks locked in my bedroom, or a Christmas convinced I was dying. I now know that, at the time, my mother and father tried to work out what might have set it off – a new baby in the house that meant we were all obsessed with sterilising and hygiene, perhaps, combined with the fact I was full of pre-pubescent hormones. They didn't have to speculate too much, thank goodness, because as quickly as my madness had appeared, it was gone again. It was, as they suspected, a phase. Just one of those funny things.

2

I think I might be normal

At this point, I feel it is really very important to stress to you that despite a childhood spent believing Father Christmas might be a sex offender, and that I was dying of AIDS, I went on to be an incredibly normal teenager. Normal, normal, normal, that's what they called me. Actually, they called me 'Bottom-of-the-bed Bryony', on account of how much I would blush when matters of a sexual nature were discussed, which led my school friends to reason that the bottom of the bed would probably be the most exotic place I ever had sex – as if my mates were erotic gymnasts who spent their weekends swinging from chandeliers at the Playboy Mansion, rather than fifteen-year-old girls who had not yet been disabused of the notion that being fingered might get them pregnant.

'What are you going to do if you get up the duff?' we all asked our most adventurous friend, Jennifer, when she announced that someone had taken her to second base. Jennifer, who had a much older sister and brother and so knew about these things, looked at us very seriously, flicked her hair and shrugged her shoulders. 'I'll cross that bridge when I come to it,' she breathed huskily, causing us all to nod at our wise, wise friend.

'IF ONLY THE GIRLS FROM SCHOOL COULD SEE ME NOW!' I wanted to holler, fifteen years later, when Bottom-of-the-bed Bryony had sex with someone behind a tree in a local park. But I didn't, because that would have been deeply unattractive, and in addition would probably have drawn attention from the park keepers, who would surely have had us done for public indecency – embarrassing at the best of times, downright shameful when the man you happen to be having sex with is married, but look, that's another chapter entirely. And anyway, any sense of adventure was soon diminished when I managed to brush my naked thigh against an angry bunch of stinging nettles, bringing me out in a violent red rash. Suddenly, it didn't seem like a terribly good story to recount at the next school reunion. 'Stick with a story about your career,' a voice in my head told me, while another screamed, 'JESUS FUCK THAT HURTS. ARE YOU COCKING INSANE, WOMAN?'

Mad Girl

But where was I? Behind a bush, desperately rummaging around in the pitch black and goodness-knows what else to find a dock leaf to rub on my naked thighs? No, no. I was being *normal.* Yes. Normal, normal, normal. Before the eating disorder, before the drugs, before the married man, before I started chanting to myself and became convinced that I was a serial-killing paedophile . . . before any of this stuff that you will in due course read about in this book, unless of course I've lost you already, I was normal. I didn't really worry all that much, or no more than the next teenager, at least. I was kind of average. Mediocre. My school reports always spoke of unlocked potential but that fact always came with the caveat that I had a sunny smile – and I did. A genuine one. I was happy, whatever that means.

I think this is very important to clarify. I think it is essential, actually, because in almost every book I have read or film I have seen, the mentally ill are tortured from the get-go, or turned that way by some terrible tragedy that befalls them. Growing up, I had this notion that there were mad people – you know, the type who shrieked like banshees in the street and banged their heads against trees – and then there was everyone else. Experience has shown me that, actually, that is not always the case. In fact, it very rarely is. Everyone has degrees of madness in them, everyone has a story to tell. If as a young woman I believed that my neuroses made me weird, I now realise, having spoken to hundreds and hundreds of seemingly ordinary people who have hidden crashing depressions and debilitating anxiety disorders, that actually these were the things that made me entirely normal.

But I am a teenager, and so despite thinking that I know everything, I am still an awfully long way off knowing anything at all. Even at thirty-five, I am still a long way off knowing anything at all. What I do know is this – I was a fantastically average adolescent. You know how in films, teenagers are either supercool and popular or misunderstood weirdos who are only ever one snarky comment away from turning a gun on everyone? Well, in reality, I think most teenagers fit in to neither of these groups, and I was no exception. If a film was to be made of my teenage years – and goodness knows I spent most of them dreaming that it would be – it would have gone straight to DVD where it would have gathered dust in the bargain bin, with no hope even of becoming a cult classic. *Mean Girls* would have become *Mediocre Girls*. I would not have merited a cameo role in *Clueless*, and it is unlikely I would ever have had *Ferris Bueller's Day Off* because I was too fearful of people in positions of authority to ever play truant. If I had, I imagine I would have done nothing more outrageous than play Super Mario Kart and read *Just Seventeen*, having first spent half an hour with my head against the radiator in order to convince my mum I actually had a temperature.

I grow up in a lovely terraced house with my sister, my brother and my mum and dad, the former being a journalist and the latter being a champagne socialist who is not too principled to send us all to private school. (These were the days when you didn't have to be an oligarch to send your kids private, although I realise that in this sense I wasn't just normal – I was remarkably fortunate.) At my all-girls school I work hard but, as I've said before, I am in no way exceptional. One year I win the Progress Cup, which is a kind of consolation prize for the decidedly average.

My only eccentricity is that I am a teenager who still sucks her thumb and has a blankie – in actual fact it is a ratty old cardigan of my mum's that I have carted around with me ever since I was two and a half. Apparently, I selected it from her wardrobe when she went in to hospital to have my sister, because the cardigan smelt of my mum and I missed her. But it's not as if I wander around at school with it; it's not as if I sit there all day with my thumb in my gob like some demented fifteen-year-old baby. Blankie – yes, this is its name – is for bedtime only, my guilty secret, and I am never teased for it. In fact, I am never bullied, and nor am I a bully. I am picked for games neither first nor last. I have a few spots, the odd blackhead, that monobrow and slightly orange hair on account of a Sun-In habit. There are glasses, after I walk into a mobility scooter – I can't even walk into a proper car, that is how dull I am – and it is decided that something should be done about my almost-permanent squint. But they are nice glasses, as opposed to the kind that Piggy wears in *Lord of the Flies*, which, by the way, is my favourite book.

I have the odd boy friend, but never a proper boyfriend. I get to snog the off-cuts that Jennifer and her cohorts are not interested in – Derek, for instance, who has his hair styled in curtains so large he is cast in perpetual darkness, which is just as well, given his habit of popping his spots.

I eventually discover tweezers and deal with the monobrow, and while in films this would be the big reveal, the moment I turn from slightly ginger geek into total megababe, in reality I just look a little less like Liam Gallagher. Anyway, nobody ever notices because my boobs are so big that nobody actually looks at my face. (My breasts are the only un-average thing about me as a teenager, and the only cause of awkward-ness I ever experience.)

I never fall in with a bad crowd. I have the odd ill-advised Malibu and Coke, and end up vomiting all over my shoes. I smoke the occasional fag, and inhale the odd exotic cheroot, as my mother will always call them, but I don't like the fuzziness, and I reason that drugs are probably not for me. I like to think of my parents popping open a bottle of wine once we had all locked ourselves in our bedrooms of an evening, and toasting each other for creating such all-round boring kids.

'Phew, what a relief!' my mum would say to my dad. 'We seem to have got away with three completely bog-standard children!'

'Yes! Despite everything, they're just so *normal*!'

My poor parents. That's all I can think. Poor, poor them.

I'm telling you all of this not to bore you to tears, but to highlight that there is absolutely no reason for anything that happens later in life to happen to me. There is no unhappy childhood, no poverty, no illness, no dodgy relatives or upheaval. We live in the same house, go on the same holidays to Spain and Cornwall, and spend all our Christmasses with much-loved cousins, aunts, uncles and grandparents. Even when my parents announce their intention to divorce, when I am twenty-one, it is not with a bang but a whimper, a sort of half-arsed shrug that says, 'We probably should have done this years ago but couldn't quite get round to it.' It's upsetting, but it is not disturbing.

I'm telling you all of this because sometimes there isn't a reason for mental illness. There isn't one at all.

Like many teenagers, the most troubling thing about my adolescence was that I was not troubled at all. My inability to stand out from a crowd, or even draw one, was deeply worrying to me. I was a girl in perpetual search of a problem, waiting endlessly for some sort of drama to happen. My teenage years had been sold to me as a dizzy time of firsts and explorations, but instead they were just one long chorus of coursework and half-arsed heartache. Teen magazines published stories about the dangers of going off the rails, but I was attached to them like a particularly stubborn tram.

There were rumours about girls at school who had drunk so much they'd ended up having their stomachs pumped, or abortions. My reaction to this unfounded tittle-tattle was not 'oh how awful' but instead 'gosh, how glamorous'. Of course, now I can think of nothing I would rather spend a weekend doing less, but when you're fifteen, getting your stomach pumped is right up there with new adidas three-stripe trainers when it comes to appearing cool.

If I thought that fretting about what I wanted to do with my life might provide me with some sort of anxiety, I was sadly mistaken. Deep down I knew. I always knew. Having grown up with a family of newspaper journalists, the printed press was the only place for me, even if my career only ever entailed making tea for stressed-out hacks. I loved the feel of a newspaper, the excitement at what was going to appear when you turned the page. I loved listening to my mum's friends, hacks the lot of them, talking about breaking stories in the newsroom and assignments that took them off to meet the world's weirdest and most wonderful people. My mother, who worked for the now defunct *Today* newspaper, had a job so far-ranging that it involved once having to feed the tigers at (the also now defunct) Windsor Safari Park; going to Moscow to cover the opening of the first McDonald's after the fall of communism; and interviewing Pavarotti. There was a giant picture of him kissing her in the middle of the spread, and for a while I was convinced they were having an affair, because obviously that was the most natural conclusion to jump to. It all seemed so impossibly exciting and fun, so different from our dull suburban existence, that I knew I had to have some part in it, too.

So I wrote. I wrote a lot. I wrote so much that I developed a bump on my right index finger – a condition that seems as dated as consumption and rickets, on account of the fact that pens are now an endangered species. And I don't want to sound like a massive ponce – this is exactly the kind of thing someone says shortly before sounding like a massive ponce – but I loved writing. I loved making forceful arguments in essays and structuring them so everything flowed and was where it should be, my ultimate goal being that the reader (massive ponce alert: by reader, I mean teacher) should reach the end without making any great effort to get there. I loved staring at a blank page – an actual blank page, not one on a screen – and wondering where I was going to go next. And at home, I loved that I could spend my evenings creating fantasy worlds and parallel universes in diaries and in notebooks, where teenage Bryony was an in-demand global superstar and not just late with her coursework.

What I didn't think about, so busy was I imagining the gasps of school friends as they discovered that I was, in fact, dating Robbie Williams after being spotted in Topshop and cast in one of his music videos, was the permanence of these fantasy worlds I constructed night after night. I didn't think about them hanging around and coming back to haunt me twenty years later. At the time I was aware of their potential to make me look like a complete and utter tit, and so I placed them in a shoebox with the words 'PRIVATE – KEEP OUT!!!!!' scrawled on it in marker pen, proving that, if nothing else, I definitely didn't have a career in security ahead of me. Then I grew up and found real dramas to occupy myself with of an evening, and forgot about them.

The year is 2015. I am thirty-five and married. I have a child and a mortgage and a family estate car in which we do the weekly shop at Sainsbury's. I am, if I say so myself, a successful columnist on a national newspaper, who gets to interview people like David

Beckham and the man who plays Poldark. I even have a book deal to write all about the many mental afflictions that have befallen me over the years, meaning I am actually going to turn my madness into something positive.

Nothing can touch me. Nothing in the world.

When I called my mum to tell her about this, she perked up considerably, a condition I mistakenly attributed to maternal pride. 'I have just the thing,' she said with a flourish. What was it? Some sort of treasured keepsake, a trinket or a bracelet perhaps, that she had kept with her during her career to bring her luck? A brand new MacBook to replace the one now covered in unidentifiable flotsam and jetsam? Even better, a ghost writer to do the book for me?

No. What she had was a large plastic box full of all the most embarrassing mementoes of my teenage years that she had collected and curated like a mortifying museum of early me. I envy teenagers nowadays, if only because they will never be reminded of what complete bellends they were, their parents probably being too digitally inept ever to work out how to break into their Facebook or hack their Snapchat (can you even hack Snapchat?). When I was a teenager, mobile phones were as rare as hen's teeth and so large that really there was nothing mobile about them at all. Social networks were not even a twinkle in anyone's eyes because the people who created the social networks were not yet twinkles in anyone's eyes. If you wanted to get in touch with friends, you had to call them on their parents' landlines, or write them a letter. Honestly, the nineties were like living in the dark ages.

Anyway, I didn't know that my mother had saved my shoebox and, even worse, had actually added to it by inserting a selection of letters written (but clearly never posted) and received, as well as embarrassing photographs of me in the aforementioned Doc Martens and Global Hypercolor T-shirts. Even at the time I had realised that these photographs were potentially morti-fying, and had ordered them to be destroyed (in those days, you couldn't just delete a photo – you had to wet the paper picture and then scratch away at the eyes). I had no idea that she had carted this flimsy box from one house to another, like a little red-spotted hankie on a stick, biding her time until the perfect moment arrived to gift me my very own Pandora's Box of horrors.

'I was going to give it to you for a special birthday,' she said, handing me the weighty box.

'I'd probably prefer a nice piece of jewellery,' I replied.

'There's no need to sound so ungrateful. There's lots of material there. It will make at least four or five pages, I'm sure.'

This is the kind of family I grew up in, one where

all personal humiliation can be used for the greater good and mined for a few hundred words.

It takes me a month to open the box. It sits in the corner of the living room, gathering dust and being climbed on by my two-year-old daughter, who would ask to be put up for adoption immediately if only she could read the contents. It taunts me, and it taunts my husband, who, worryingly, likes nothing more than amassing reasons for why he shouldn't have married me.

'I think you'll feel better once you've opened it,' he says one evening.

'I think *you'll* feel better once I've opened it.'

'I mean, I could do with a laugh, obviously. But mostly I just want you to be able to move on.'

'I *have* moved on! I'm thirty-five and only occasionally fantasise about a parallel universe where I'm married to a handsome Hollywood A-lister!'

'Who?'

'You see! This box has caused nothing but problems, and I haven't even opened it yet. You're already wondering which handsome actor I might want to have an affair with. Just imagine what carnage will ensue once I prise open the lid. I'm sure I could have written this book perfectly well without it, but now my mum's plonked it in my head I'm convinced it's completely integral to the whole thing.'

'I can guarantee you're going to feel better once you've opened it.'

'I can guarantee that I'll feel worse.'

'Sometimes you have to feel worse to feel better. It's like tidying a bedroom.'

'How can you compare writing a book to tidying a bedroom? And what would you know about either of those things?'

Anyway, I open the box eventually, and it is not nearly as bad as I imagined it. No, it is far, far worse. It is like thinking you are a bit skint and discovering you have been defrauded of all your life-savings, or going in for a routine doctor's check-up only for the bloods to reveal you have a terminal illness. That is to say, before my mum turned up with this bloody box, I thought I was a bit of a numpty, but afterwards, I realise that I was actually a class-A cretin.

Take, for example, the imaginary magazine profile I wrote of myself, inside a green notebook. The title on the front proclaims: BRYONY GORDON'S FUNKY THOUGHTS (1996). The imaginary magazine profile has the headline 'FRIENDS OF THE STAR', which I have underlined painstakingly with a ruler not once, not twice, but three times, in a crude attempt at making it look like a proper feature. And the standfirst . . . well, the standfirst is something else:

When 17-year-old [I must have been gazing into my crystal ball, as in 1996 I was sixteen tops] *Bryony Gordon was cast in the cult film of '97 with Brad Pitt and David Duchovny* [WTF?], *she went from schoolgirl to superstar. And her friends watched her every step of the way. XX* [insert actual journalist's name here, cribbed from the pages of some newspaper supplement] *meets them. Photographs by XXX* [insert actual photographer's name here, also cribbed from the pages of some newspaper supplement].

It gets worse. I know that seems impossible, but really, it does. Marvel at the masterly way in which I manage to make myself sound like a hateful fucking douchebag in the actual 'copy'.

Bryony Gordon has lots of friends. And they're all here. [What is this? Some sort of teenybopper version of *This Is Your Life?*] *Says one: 'I remember the time this fat business bloke approached her in the pub* [what was I doing in the pub? I was underage!]. *We all thought, 'Sleaze! He's going to try it on with her.' But he was a big film executive* [what was he doing in this imaginary pub?] *and he said he wanted her in his film in America. She never wanted to be an actress, let alone famous!'*

For the director [insert name of actual film director cribbed from review section of newspaper], *this was more than a stroke of luck. He had found a beauty with amazing acting abilities* [I had never even been in a school nativity]. *Soon, Bryony was on a plane to New York to meet her co-stars, Duchovny and Pitt. 'She always loved watching films but she never wanted to act,' said another friend.* [Yes, we got that earlier, 'friend'.] *'Whenever xxx* [insert name of boy I had once snogged whose dad had produced a biscuit ad] *started to talk about the film industry, she'd just laugh. Look at her now. She really is laughing.'*

Sadly, this imaginary magazine profile was cut short, perhaps by an imaginary magazine editor shouting 'that's enough self-absorption – ed', so it is unclear to the reader of this particular article what happened when I got to New York and met my co-stars, Pitt and Duchovny. Thankfully – or not, depending on whether you happen to be me or someone else entirely – another imaginary magazine piece a few pages later gives us some hint as to what came next. This time, the head-line reads 'LONG DISTANCE LOVE' (no neat under-lining this time, perhaps because this imaginary magazine feature had been commissioned with a 'softer' angle). The standfirst is another masterpiece in how not write a standfirst:

They've caused a scandal because of their age gap, listened to the media lecture them about how their rela-tionship is doomed, and endured a handful of exes uncov-ering their sex secrets. But two years on, Bryony Gordon is still together with David Duchovny.

I mean, there are lots of points to make here, aren't there? Almost too many to mention in a book that is supposed to be only 80,000 words long. Who were these exes who had discussed my sex secrets, given

41

that at this stage, I had had brief, perfunctory sex just once in my life? And why, if I was playing make-believe, had I limited it to just a handful of exes? Did I think that a handful of exes in my past was a respectable number? And who measures sexual partners in handfuls, other than people who should be in prison?

But most importantly, why, when given the choice between the most handsome man ever to have walked the earth and David Duchovny, did I choose David Duchovny?

I was basically playing with myself, I guess (no, not like that), using my biro to create worlds I would previously have created with some Sylvanian Families or a Barbie doll. But still, it's embarrassing. Almost as bad are the letters I wrote to Childline, but never sent, as even I must have realised that they were completely ridiculous.

Dear Esther Rantzen,

I've just been through a lot. This is a very emotional letter. You see I was completely stuck on my maths homework, and I still am, and I was complaining to my mum about it. I started to cry, and then Jack (my dad) came home, and told me to go to my room and took my maths file. I screamed and shouted, claiming that now I would get bad marks at school, and that would just add to my reputation of bad marks. I called my dad a bastard and all sorts of things and I collected

*my papers and ran upstairs. But he didn't even come
and see me. Neither of them did.*

*It was very upsetting, seeing as I am really going
through a hard time at school.*

From,

Bryony

And

Dear Esther Rantzen,

*This is a hard letter to write and it has taken me
a lot of courage. My mum has had a new baby and
now I think she hates me and even my sister. She is
always telling us to be quiet as the baby is sleeping
but are we supposed to just stop with our lives because
of him? What does he matter anyway, he is only six
months old? I don't know what to do, I think she
will never love us again.*

From,

Bryony

There are other missives in there, from a boy I had
completely forgotten about whom I must have had a
crush on for about two weeks one summer. These are
so mortifying I feel I have to share them with you, if
only to share some of the mortification – to offload it
onto you.

Mad Girl

Dear Bryony,

When I read your letter I felt like bursting into tears. What you had done was poured out all your emotions concerning me on one page [cool, Bryony, cool!] *and that touched me coz it shows how much of a courageous person you are. A lot of people having to deal with the type of shit that society and even yourself have dumped on your shoulders would have snapped ages ago and reached for the pistol, razor, aspirins etc. But I know you, Bryony. You have become the best friend anyone could have.* [Urggh, the friend line.] *You cannot pick up that pistol* [where the hell would I even get a pistol?], *put the barrel against your head and end it. Let me tell you it's not worth it. You have got more friends than the richest man in the world. I know that if you were to end your life, then I would be next. I would follow you to oblivion because I value your presence on this earth more than a lot of things. I value you among the most wonderful things in life, as one of the finest human specimens ever to walk the cursed mother earth.*

Your friend with you forever and eternity.

XX [Name changed to protect the guilty]

PS You don't ever have to be sorry, Bryony Gordon.

PPS Our little group has always been and always will until THE END.

I have only the haziest of recollections of what prompted this letter – him turning me down during a night on the hooches, the kind of thing I would soon come to accept, but that at the time was cause for hysterical hand-wringing and angst, even, possibly – horrifically – proclamations that I wanted to end my own life. I cannot even ask the boy who wrote it for the particulars, because despite his promises that our little group would always be until THE END, I have not seen him since I was eighteen.

You know when people write letters to their fifteen-year-old selves, revealing what they wish they'd known then? If I had to write one, I would say this: don't spend your teenage years waiting for something to happen. Count yourself lucky, enjoy the banality. Remember that there is plenty of time to shine. Stop craving drama. And be careful what you wish for.

3

I think I might have killed
someone

The doctor's surgery I have gone to from birth has not changed since my two-week weigh-in. That's what my mother tells me, as we sit in the brown plastic seats bolted to the floor, staring at the brown walls and the brown tables covered in magazines that are only two years out of date, as opposed to seventeen years, if what my mother says is true.

'Even the receptionist is the same,' she says, pointing to the harassed-looking woman leafing through medical records. She must get ill a lot, I think. She must have a year-long cold, a constant cough, be a frequent sufferer of the flu. If you put her under a giant microscope, I bet her skin would light up and actually crawl with all the germs and bacteria, transferred by the hacking, spluttering people she is forced to come into contact with every day. How can she stand it, I wonder? How can she bear to be here with all this disease and pestilence?

My mother picks up one of the aged, dog-eared magazines and idly starts to flick through it. I am appalled by her nonchalance, repulsed even. 'Don't,' I say. 'Please don't.' For the briefest of moments she looks confused, irritated even, but she soon remembers and puts it down. Then she does the only thing she can in the situation. She changes the subject.

She jokes about all her memories of this surgery – the handsome doctor that the mothers in her antenatal group would make up illnesses to see; how as a toddler, I had hated the ice-cold feel of the stethoscope, and had to be bribed with sweets to let the doctor anywhere near me, despite his handsomeness; the time that Dad had thrown a stick for the dog in the park and it had hit Mum instead and when she went in with a black eye, they all gave her a look that said, 'Sure, of course you were out walking the dog.'

Did I remember the time when my brother Rufus had managed to get his hands on the delicious pink medicine, i.e. the Calpol, and sat down on the stairs where he politely poured the contents into a glass and drank it, like an old woman taking tea? And the relief when the doctor announced he was just below the toxicity levels so would be fine, if a little wonky for a few hours? For that matter, did I recall the time when Naomi drank several litres of swimming-pool water on a Sunday afternoon in an attempt to make herself sick to get the day off school, only for it to work a little too well?

Yes, I nod robotically, yes I do.

Of course, says Mum, as I pull my coat up over my mouth to avoid the germs of the surgery, of course the absolute worst thing was when I was sent home from school with terrible stomach pain, and she had to come back from work to take me to the doctor.

'Do you remember,' asks Mum, 'what I said to you as I drove you here?'

I nod silently.

'I said to you, "If you are faking this to get a day off school, you will be in BIG trouble."'

I nod silently.

'And then two hours later you were being wheeled into theatre at the Charing Cross Hospital to have your appendix out!'

I nod silently.

'You were only eight! Off school for almost a month, nil by mouth, the works! They thought you might have got blood poisoning because it was about to burst!'

She says it like it was all a jolly adventure.

I nod silently.

'And what about when you turned yellow and kept falling asleep, and we came here and the doctor said to you, "Do you use intravenous drugs?" I mean, you were fifteen! And even if you were using intravenous drugs, as if you were going to tell him in front of me!'

I nod silently.

'And then he said he had checked your arms for track marks but there weren't any, so that was a relief, until of course I asked why he had asked if you were a smack addict, and he said that you were jaundiced, which suggested liver disease. Liver disease, at fifteen!'

I nod silently.

'But it turned out you just had glandular fever, so that was something.'

She finishes her romp through my medical history just as the doctor calls my name. And I think to myself, 'The appendicitis I could deal with, because it only required an operation. The glandular fever was fine, because it made me seem cool on account of the fact you are supposed to catch it through snogging. But how am I going to get through the next fifteen minutes? How am I going to tell my mum, let alone the doctor, what is happening? How am I going to explain to them that my head keeps telling me I have killed someone?'

For five completely uneventful years (bar the glandular fever), I take the same route back from the tube station to our house after school. It involves boring residential roads, a parade of useless shops, which I now realise were probably fronts for money-laundering operations, and a short, badly lit alleyway that, during the winter months, I am instructed to run down screaming while dispensing pepper spray into the air, doling out karate kicks as I go.

All in all, the walk takes about fifteen, twenty minutes tops – and less after the clocks go back, thanks to the teenage assassin act I am forced to carry out. I fill that time listening to my Walkman and imagining myself in the videos of my favourite songs (in the summer months), and perfecting stand-up comedy routines that nobody will ever hear (in the winter months). It is the perfect backdrop to my teenage years – dull and predictable, with promises of drama that are never quite fulfilled.

But as my A-levels approach, the walk takes on a more menacing tone. The clocks have sprung forward, the evenings are lighter, the air is balmier, the end is within sight (well, the end of school, that is) and yet something isn't quite right. No. That doesn't quite cover it. Something seems very, very wrong. I can't quite put my finger on it, can't trace the sense of unease, but I start to become uncomfortable on my little walk home. The most tedious journey in the world suddenly feels threatening. It doesn't feel safe. Not because I am scared of what some stranger might do to me but because I am scared of what I might do to some stranger.

Your parents warn you about the monsters you might

encounter in dark alleyways, but they never warn you about the monsters you might find in your own mind, the ones that taunt and trouble you, and make you question yourself to your very core. It is the April before I take my A-levels, the cruellest month, according to T.S. Eliot, and yet I can't help but wonder if I am not the cruellest thing of all. I can't help but wonder if my run-of-the-mill, middle-class life hides something darker, something more desperate. I can't help but wonder if I am who I think I am.

'They wouldn't hurt a fly,' is what people say, isn't it? But I really wouldn't, much to the bemusement of my sister, who likes nothing more than watching insects die slow, painful deaths after being napalmed with an extra large can of Raid. A mosquito would have to turn me into one giant, screaming scab before I even considered trying to swat it with a magazine. When it rains and the snails come out, I move them off paths so they aren't crushed underfoot. I dislike harm coming to all creatures great and small – not because I am a good, decent human being who detests pain and suffering so much it actually causes me pain and suffering, but because I am scared that if I hurt anything else, karma will ensure that, ultimately, I will get hurt too. I am an egotistical altruist, if you will.

So it is acutely disturbing to me that, on my walk home, I start to notice rubbish bins I could dump clothes in, and grit bins I could dump bodies in. Why have I never before paid any attention to that bit of the alleyway under the railway bridge, the haven for graffiti artists and perhaps the odd homeless person? Wouldn't this be exactly the kind of place one might lay in wait to kidnap someone, if one was that way inclined? And was I that way inclined? Was I, was I, was I?

The smallest slither of suggestion lodges itself in my mind – might I have killed someone and blanked it from my memory? I can't explain it, do not know where it has come from or why it is there, but there it unmistakeably is. I am seventeen and on the cusp of university and real life, but my brain swims with a very different type of possibility, the kind they don't tell you about in careers lessons. 'Miss Gordon, your teachers say you show a great aptitude for criminality. Have you ever thought about a career in kidnapping or murdering?' Every bone in my body says no, no, NO, DO NOT BE SO RIDICULOUS, but my brain will not listen to the bones in my body. It sticks its fingers in its ears and point blank refuses to acknowledge that they are even there in the first place, screaming, 'LALALALALALA, I CAN'T HEAR YOU!'

Everywhere I look, the most ordinary things, things I scarcely noticed before, suddenly seem menacing. They spring to life but promise only death. Knife blocks and curtain cords are to be kept away from at all costs because they are potential murder weapons. Bleach, too – I might pour it in my drink, or worse, someone else's. I start to count paracetamol tablets, counting being a way of checking that I haven't crushed up a load to sprinkle in my sister's food. If there are two or three or four fewer than the day before, a cold panic grips me. 'Have you been having headaches?' I ask my family at the dinner table, as a way of establishing that there is a perfectly reasonable explanation for the disappearance of the tablets. There is, there always is, but that doesn't stop the anxiety. It just sets it down a different path, in search of some other worry to attach itself to: carbon monoxide, for example, seeping silently and odourlessly out of your boiler, shutting down your body without you even realising.

The world as I know it is crumpling in on itself and I do not know why. I do not know why, and I do not know how to put it back together again, although I try, I really do try. In an attempt to take back control of my head, I develop rituals. I have no idea that in doing this, I am making everything much, much worse. I fret obsessively about the wellbeing of my five-year-old brother, and begin to utter offerings to the universe to keep him safe – 'I would rather I died than him, I would rather I died than him, I would rather I died than him' – over and over and over again in case I accidentally get it wrong. I cannot get it wrong, because then I cannot keep him safe.

Soon, one phrase becomes two. Then two become

three. Before long, I am spending most of the day muttering to myself.

I would rather I died than any of my family.

I would never hurt anyone.

I will not go to prison.

I do not deserve to be in prison.

The Gordons are happy and healthy and will all live to old age.

Everyone is happy and healthy.

Nobody has a terminal illness.

Please take me and not them.

And so on and so on.

I scour the news for reports of gruesome crimes, to check that I do not recognise in them some deep-rooted desire in myself. Reading them is an ordeal that I feel I have to go through as punishment for the thoughts in my head. The words 'rape' and 'murder' send me into a tailspin, and have to be replaced with the continued chanting of several other, happy ones (note: not positive, since this has associations with HIV). Care. Hug. Love. Not comfort. Comfort is what you do when someone has died.

Tics start to overtake me. For some reason – and reader, I still don't understand this, almost twenty years on – I have to say my happy words if I drop something on the floor. I have to say them when I am plucking my eyebrows and when I go up the first three steps of the staircase from the landing. I have to say them when I touch my pillow and when my fingers come into contact with the latch on the garage door. All of these actions, I must repeat again and again, the happy words going through my head all along, just to ensure I get everything right because otherwise . . . what, exactly? What would happen if I didn't make myself look like a demented mime artist every time I went to open the garage door?

In an attempt to prove to myself that I am not a potential killer, I try to imagine killing someone. While most teenagers lie in bed dreaming of crushes, I lie there checking my body's reactions to the image in my head that involves me strangling, or stabbing, someone. My body's reaction is always the same – pure, unadulterated horror. But any relief at this horror is short-lived, replaced almost instantly by different questions, such as surely the very act of trying to imagine killing someone is enough to make me a potential killer? Surely this makes me a bit . . . well, *wrong*?

When I masturbate, which given I am a seventeen-year-old girl, is often, terrible images flash into my head unbidden – images of children playing in parks, or walking to school. It is horrific, a real passion killer. 'I only like GROWN ADULTS' I will chant for the next hour, in order to convince the world that as well as not being a psychotic murderer, I am also not a paedophile. Alone in my room, I tug at my hair in disgust. I hit my scalp in horror and pinch my skin as

55

punishment. I want to pull at my head, and replace it with a new one.

And on and on it seems to go, this endless cycle of self-loathing and despair.

Exam stress. That's what this is. Good old-fashioned exam stress. At school, everyone is sitting in the library muttering to themselves under their breath. Plus, there's one girl who is as thin as the pencil she constantly chews on, which, by the way, is the only thing anyone has seen her chew on for the last three months. She is the perfect foil for my madness. Compared with her, I look positively normal. Not to mention fat.

At home, the muttering and the paracetamol counting is, in retrospect, probably a little more obvious, although at the time I am convinced I have managed to hide it from everyone. Not my mum, of course. She's a mother, after all, her intuition as finely tuned as the most sophisticated military radar. And so it is that one Thursday evening, after she has been to the cinema with my dad and I have spent a fraught few hours checking over and over again that my brother is still breathing, she comes to my room and starts to tell me about the film she has just seen. It is called *As Good As It Gets*, and it has won lots of awards, not least for its star, Jack Nicholson, thanks to his portrayal of a man with something called obsessive compulsive disorder.

'It's more commonly known as OCD,' explains my mother, who has perched herself at the end of my bed. Please bear in mind that the year is 1998, and that OCD has yet to become the celebrity illness *du jour*. It has yet to become shorthand for saying 'I like to live in a clean flat', which, when you think about it, is something that barely needs stating, because who likes living in filth? But anyway. This was before TV stars would sit on breakfast-show sofas and say, 'Oh, I'm a bit OCD when it comes to my home. You should see my sock drawer!' So I have no idea what OCD is, and don't much care given that there are more pressing things to worry about, like whether or not I am a serial killer. But there my mum is, sitting at the end of my bed, boring me with the-interesting-thing-she-has-learnt-at-the-cinema, and I just want her to go away.

I look at her with typical teenage disdain. Why is she telling me this? Can she not see that I have revision to do, or pretend revision, which actually involves me staring at a page while I forensically repeat my walk home in my head, checking it did not involve murder or child abuse? What do I even care about the stupid dumb film she has just been to see starring some old Hollywood fogey?

She reads my mind, and presents me with a piece she has torn out from the *Guardian* newspaper.

'I think you might find this interesting. I think you

might find the film interesting. Anyway, have a read, and let me know.'

She kisses me on the head and thanks me for looking after my siblings. 'Thank you for not killing your siblings,' a voice in my head says to me. Then she leaves me alone with my thoughts, and the crumpled piece of newspaper.

The article is all about obsessive compulsive disorder, the illness everyone is talking about after Nicholson jokily skipped up the steps to collect his Oscar, carefully avoiding cracks as he went. As I will learn again and again as I get older, OCD is really funny if you don't actually happen to suffer from it. Anyway, OCD, it explains, is an often debilitating condition that causes sufferers to have intrusive thoughts (obsessions) that they try to calm with certain rituals (compulsions). Saying phrases, for example, or repeatedly washing their hands. Sufferers know that their actions are not rational, but feel powerless to stop them. And yet the more they carry them out, the worse their condition gets.

OCD, explains the article, can take many forms. Some sufferers fear being contaminated, while others become preoccupied with the idea of harm coming to those they love. Some might fear they are gay because an image of their best friend pops into their head while having sex, while others become anxious that they are child molesters because of inappropriate thoughts while surrounded by young people. Almost everyone has these inappropriate thoughts, says the piece – what if I dropped this baby or pushed this person under a train or pictured my colleagues without their clothes on? – but almost everyone dismisses them because they realise they are just part of the brain's randomness, and not a sign that anything is actually wrong with them. But people with OCD cannot dismiss these thoughts. They cling to them, and fret about them, and become upset by them. Although their eyes can see that they are not a murderer or a paedophile and that there isn't dirt on their hands or gas coming out of the oven, their brains refuse to acknowledge it. OCD, the article explains, is often called the 'doubting disease' because it makes sufferers question even the most basic things about themselves. It doesn't matter how unlikely something is, OCD will worm its way in and find the slimmest shred of evidence that it could happen, and then blow it up out of all proportion. Sufferers are risk averse to the point that they lock themselves away in their own heads. OCD, concludes the article, is not just a jokey condition played for laughs in a Hollywood film, but a serious disorder that affects about 1.2 per cent of the population.

I read the piece over and over again: 1.2, 1.2, 1.2. I chant it to myself, like a soothing prayer.

I think I might be part of the 1.2.

The tears flow, working on me like sedatives. I pass out that night feeling strangely relieved and more than a little bit sorry for myself. I am not a murderer, after all! I am just ill!

But by the time I wake up in the morning, my brain is back to its old tricks again. As I soon learn, OCD thrives on relief. Relief is its breeding ground, the place in which it produces more anxieties and worries. And now I have the most meta worry of all, which is how can I be entirely sure that I actually have OCD? How do I know that I'm not clinging on to everything in this article in some desperate attempt at exonerating myself? Can't you just imagine the scene in court? I certainly can. *'The defendant claims that she would never act on these murderous thoughts in her head, that they are not impulses but merely the result of a mental illness known as Obsessive Compulsive Disorder.' The prosecution pauses for effect. The jury looks serious, while the defendant's lawyer puts her head in her hands. 'But I put it to you that this is nothing more than a wicked lie concocted by the defendant to cover up crimes conducted while pretending to be an ordinary schoolgirl with a disorder caused by exam stress. I put it to you that far from being a vulnerable seventeen-year-old breaking under the pressure of too many coursework deadlines, the defendant is actually a cold, calculating MONSTER!'*

The jury gasps. The defendant wails. Her mother breaks down in tears, while her sister mouths the word 'LOSER' at the dock, where the defendant is being dragged away by police guards after the judge decrees that for the first time in legal history, she should be locked up without further trial, with the guards then throwing away the key.

I pull myself back to reality. This can't go on. I shower and dress for school and creep out the front door without saying goodbye to anyone. And then I make the walk to the tube station, wondering what my mum will think when she finds the note in her handbag, the one that simply says: 'I think we need to go to the doctor. x'.

The GP is, like most GPs, harassed-looking and to the point. I notice, as he invites us to sit down, that his tie has tiny pigs on it that could be mistaken for polka dots were you not the kind of person who is desperate to focus on anything other than the screwed-up voices inside your own head. 'Nice pigs,' I say quietly, but he is too busy rifling through my medical notes to hear.

'So what can I help you with this afternoon?' he says, bright and breezy and as if he is taking orders for tea. I make a long 'ummmmm' noise and feel my chest tighten again. 'Well,' I think to myself. 'You could help me work out if I am murderer or just plain mad. You could help me with the fact I can no longer get myself a glass of water because what if I accidentally filled it with bleach instead? You could help me with the fact that every time I see a child, it feels like my brain has been plunged into a cauldron of terror? You could help me to go to sleep for a month so I don't have to think or worry or fret.'

But instead I just burst into tears.

I had put on mascara before coming here, as if this might make me appear more normal. Now, as it runs down my face, I look anything but. The doctor hands me some tissues from a box on his desk, which I accept not gratefully but fearfully, stuffing them in my jacket pocket in case they are covered in germs.

My mum puts her arm around me and tries to explain what she has gleaned from my increasingly erratic behaviour.

'We first thought Bryony might have something wrong with her when she was about eleven or twelve, and she washed her hands obsessively, but then it went away and we just put it down to a phase.'

I look up at her, completely startled. It had never occurred to me to link the two until now. I had almost forgotten about that strange period of my pre-pubescence.

'But in the last couple of months, we've noticed that she has gone from being a bubbly young girl to one who is quite withdrawn. She has A-level exams coming up so she's under a lot of pressure and . . .'

'I think I have OCD,' I blurt out to the doctor, unable to bear the fact that my mother has been quietly assessing me. It is like discovering that friends have been gossiping about me behind my back. 'When I was younger I was scared I had AIDS and now I am scared that I will hurt someone even though I can't think of anything I would rather do less. It's plaguing me every waking hour and I don't want to feel like this any more. I think I need some sort of help. I can't take it any more.'

The doctor nods, as if I have just described to him something totally normal, the symptoms of a chest infection, perhaps, or a mild dose of the flu. The fact he hasn't picked up his phone and called through to the woman on reception for help is mildly comforting to me; clearly he does not see me as anything other than a bit pathetic. Indeed, his reaction gives me the slightest glimmer of hope, one that just this morning would have seemed impossible. Suddenly I am seeing myself through this stranger's eyes, and I do not see a dangerous psychopath. I just see someone who is lost in the fog of mental illness.

'It does sound to me like OCD,' says the doctor, who is now bobbing his head up and down like a nodding dog. 'Do you have little rituals that you have to carry out to keep yourself and others safe?'

'Ahuh,' I say, starting to cry again.

'Do you have to do things until they are just right?'

'Yes.'

'Do you have unwanted thoughts that disturb you but which you cannot get rid of?'

The sound I make is a strangulated one.

'And this has been going on for how long?'

'It feels like forever.' I stare at the pigs again, and note that they are also wearing ties and bowler hats, which they hold cheerfully at jaunty angles. 'But it's probably been a couple of months.'

'I think it is likely that you are suffering from OCD and as a result of that I would say you are probably also experiencing clinical depression.' Clinical depression. I try the words out for size, and almost laugh to myself at the ridiculousness of the term – there has been nothing clinical about the way I have felt recently.

My mum puts her hand over her mouth and starts shaking her head. I can see what she is thinking. She is thinking, 'How could I not have known for so long? How could I have let this happen?' I feel sorry for her, really I do, but right now the pigs can't stop dancing in front of me.

'It's OK, Mum,' I say, because now I am sitting here in front of the doctor and his tie full of pigs, I feel saved, I feel released, I feel that everything is about to be made better. I feel like the lone survivor of a shipwreck, washing up on an island after a month at sea, carried to safety by a kindly group of people who will feed, water and bathe me back to health. Suddenly, I remember what it is like to feel good.

'I tell you what I think we should do,' says the doctor. Now I am nodding along, keen to get to his solution, the drugs he is going to put me on, the therapy he is going to sign me up for.

'I think what we should do, because of your age, is wait for, say, three weeks, and if you're not feeling any better, we should think about putting you on a course of antidepressants. In the meantime, if things get worse, please come back immediately.'

He stands up and goes to open the door. I find myself walking towards it, vaguely hear my mother say, 'Thank you, doctor,' and before I can even register what has happened, we are back in the brown waiting room, walking through it to the car, me speechless, my mum keen to get us out of there without anyone noticing the mascara all over my face. And all I can think is, 'Three weeks. Three weeks. THREE. FUCKING. WEEKS.' If at that moment a minute feels like an hour and an hour like a day – and that's what time feels like when you are suffering from a mental illness – how am I going to deal with almost a month?

I get into the car and once the door is closed and nobody but my mother can hear I become completely disconsolate. My face is a pasty, puffed-up mess of mucus and Maybelline. This is worse than the time Simon North asked me on a date only to cancel half an hour before.

'It's like learning the family house is worth a million quid,' I snort to my mother, 'only for it to fall down the next day ON ALL YOUR CHILDREN.' Having plucked up the courage to go to the doctor, having been reassured that – hallelujah! – I am mentally ill and not a murdering maniac, having put myself within touching distance of a way to quieten the unbearable noise in my head . . . well, the best the doctor can tell me to do is wait. Do nothing. Hope that it will pass, just like the episode before.

I cannot remember precisely what I said to my mother in that car park, but we both agree that it was something along the lines of: I will NOT wait, and I will NOT do nothing. I have tried to make this go away by myself but all that has happened is it's got louder and larger. I cannot think about how I will feel three hours from now, let alone three weeks. I need to do something RIGHT THIS VERY MINUTE.

So we get out of the car and walk back into the brown waiting room, which, despite looking the same for almost twenty years, suddenly feels very different from how it did just half an hour before. And my mum stands with me at the reception, and she says to the woman there, 'The doctor told us to come back if it got worse. Well, it just did.' And ten minutes later I leave Dr Pig-Tie with a prescription in my hand, my name on a psychologist's waiting list, and a feeling that I am now armed for battle.

It's just as well I do not know that I will be back, if not to this doctor's surgery, then to another. I will be back again and again and again.

4

I think my hair might be falling out

It is, I now realise, quite a big deal to put a child on antidepressants, even if that child is seventeen. At the beginning of 2016, a report published in the *British Medical Journal* found that teenagers who take the most common forms of the drugs – Prozac, Seroxat, Zoloft, Effexor and Cymbalta – have a doubled risk of aggression or suicidal behaviour. And we are constantly hearing that too many people, of all ages, are prescribed 'happy pills' – as they are often flippantly described – with use doubling in the last decade according to the NHS Health and Social Care Information Centre, so that there are almost as many prescriptions given out annually as there are people in the country (57 million dispensed by chemists in England and Wales in 2014).

Can that many of us really be properly depressed? Are we all being drugged by evil Big Pharma companies? Should we not just be 'pulling ourselves together'?

My opinion, and it is only my opinion, is that if you're feeling so bad you find yourself in a doctor's surgery, then certainly you should consider a prescription of antidepressants if it is handed out to you. But be aware that some forms of the drug work better for certain mental-health conditions than others, and know that some people feel spaced out on them. (Side note: I never have. The only thing I've ever noticed is a drop in libido.) They are also a bitch to come off. Honestly. They are that girl at school you secretly hoped would get pregnant by her hunky boyfriend and shipped off in shame. I always know when I have forgotten to take mine for a couple of days because I start to get a surreal feeling every time I turn my head, like I am being zapped with a stun gun. I am tired and listless and find it very difficult to concentrate. Then I take a tablet and – ping! – everything is OK again almost immediately. Of course, the fact you can go cold turkey from antidepressants is precisely the reason some people are so against them, and I do see that point of view, really I do. But for me, the alternative is not an option. Like Chernobyl or Fukushima, it is not a place I am keen to explore.

I have spent much of my adult life going on and off antidepressants as if they're sweets, before finally deciding three years ago that they are just a form of medication I need to take, like an asthmatic needing an inhaler or a diabetic needing insulin. Depression, after all, is an illness like any other, and it's not even close to being on the same scale as the really 'shameful' ones, such as syphillis, or gonorrhea, so why the feeling of failure when it comes to taking drugs for it? You are not a failure. You are quite the opposite, because you are trying to do something to make yourself better. Depression isn't going to make your genitalia go crusty and fall off, or at least not directly anyway. So when it comes to medication, why do mental illnesses get off scot-free, while all other diseases are treated and managed? Why are they allowed to roam around our bodies causing destruction and mayhem without any intervention? And if we allow them to do this, are we not contributing to the unhelpful but all-pervading belief that when it comes to matters of the mind, 'things will just get better'? Yes, they may well do, but when, exactly? In a few days' time? In a month? In a couple of years? And what are you supposed to do, or not do, while you're waiting around for your mental illness to clear up? Sit there in your flat all day, in the dark, with the curtains drawn, refusing to see anyone and hoping that you don't get sacked from your job? Are you supposed to put everything on hold until the moment your illness decides to go away? Imagine that I was talking about someone with a chest infection instead of depression and you would wonder why on earth they weren't taking something to make them feel better. But for some reason we find such a lackadaisical approach perfectly normal when it comes to our mental health. In some cases, it is not just normal, it is seen as preferable to taking action. And that really is mental.

But back to being seventeen. The leaflet that accompanies the antidepressant I have been prescribed is roughly the same length as *War and Peace*, and as literature it is just as daunting. The potential list of side effects are all things you would want to avoid at your most happy, let alone when you happen to be feeling pretty low. There are complaints I do not even know exist, despite reading medical encyclopedias for symptoms of AIDS in my early adolescent years. Vaginal haemorrhage, toxic epidermal necrolysis, red painful penis, tooth disorder, tongue disorder – these are just a few of the things listed under the very long part of the leaflet marked 'possible side effects'.

I sit on my bed and gawp at all the things these pills I am about to take might do to me. Anorexia, increased appetite (as I get older, I will learn that antidepressant leaflets have an impressive knack of heaping things together that happen to be the complete opposite of each other), depression (hello? What is the point of taking a pill for depression that could potentially make you more depressed?), feeling strange, nightmares, anxiety, lack of attention, numbness and tingling, shaking, visual disturbance, palpitations, abdominal pain, vomiting, constipation, upset stomach, gas, rash, increased sweating, sexual dysfunction, erectile dysfunction, hallucination, feeling too happy (that's the whole point, antidepressants, that's the whole point), lack of caring (that too), convulsion, involuntary muscle contractions, abnormal coordination, moving a lot, amnesia, speech disorder, migraine, ear pain, high blood pressure, breathing difficulty, nose bleed, excessive vaginal bleed, inflammation of the oesophagus, haemorrhoids, burping, eye swelling, hair loss, cold sweat, dry skin, hives, osteoarthritis, back pain, nighttime urination, unable to urinate, increase in urination, increase in frequency of urination, problem urinating, female sexual dysfunction, malaise, chills, fever, weakness, thirst, weight decrease, weight increase, intestine problem (do you want to be any more specific there?), ear infection, CANCER, high cholesterol, drug dependence, psychotic disorder, aggression, suicidal thoughts, sleep walking, blood in stool, sore mouth, skin problem with blisters, hair rash (WTF?), skin odour abnormal, bone disorder, urinary incontinence (please not more urine), urinary hesitation (OK then), prolonged erection, breast discharge, hernia, abnormal laboratory tests, injury (any old one will do), decrease in white blood cells, low thyroid hormones, endocrine problem, diabetes, skin oedema, menstrual irregularities, breast enlargement, passing out, bedwetting, serious liver function problems, swelling in legs, an increased risk of bone fractures, terrifying abnormal dreams (why is this the one that gets to me the most?).

So, basically, everything. That's what this leaflet is saying to me: take these pills and you run the risk of suffering from every medical condition that has ever been diagnosed, and a fair few that haven't. Eat me, and you're going down the rabbit hole. And they call this medication? Dudes, medication is supposed to make you get better, not worse!

But I don't care. If I weigh up the risks in my head, I would rather my vagina haemorrhaged or I started to wet the bed than I continue to feel the way I do. At that moment, I would rather have osteoarthritis than OCD. So I sweep the leaflet to one side, pick up the glass of water on my bedside table, pop the pill out of its wrapping, and take my first-ever antidepressant.

The doctor has told me that it will take some time before I feel the effects of the drugs, that things could actually get worse before they get better, but that night I go to bed feeling calm and safe and like maybe, possibly, everything is going to be OK. I go to bed with hope. And hope, as anyone who has been in the grips of a mental illness will know, is often in very short supply. It is not just in short supply – it is extinguished. It's not that you don't dare to have it; it's that you've forgotten it ever existed. I don't mean this offensively, don't want you to think I'm trying to kick people while they are down, but when you are bang in the middle of a mental illness, you really are 'hopeless'.

So for me, the drug's effect kicks in immediately. Every day, I wake up feeling a bit better than the one before. Yes, I know that's what we call a placebo effect. But it's still an effect, isn't it? It's still a change from feeling like crap. Maybe I would have started to feel better anyway. Maybe some forms of mental illness hit a natural peak and then start to ebb away slowly after that. But maybe the antidepressants give me the kick-start I so desperately need. And I do not want to know what would have happened without them.

The therapist that I eventually see, several months after my appointment with the GP, is a man my mother finds privately when it becomes clear that I am getting no nearer to the end of the NHS waiting list. He works out of a room so miserable that simply looking at it makes me want to pop a Valium. This, I will eventually learn, seems to be the default interior design for therapists. Yellow walls. Black floors. No windows. Barely any air. Chairs so uncomfortable that even through layers of fat you can feel the bones in your bottom. Not a sofa or chaise longue in sight, despite what the movies will have you believe. I imagine that when they are training, there's a module taught by some bleak, Soviet-era architect-cum-designer who warns them if

73

they do not follow his advice, they will be struck off immediately. It's as if at the dawn of therapy-time, Sigmund Freud sat down and thought, 'What's the best place to treat people experiencing persistent sadness, lethargy and anxiety? I know, a really depressing room with no natural light!' And from then on, everyone has taken his lead without ever stopping to question it because they're all too busy wondering if they've got an Oedipus complex.

The therapist is quiet and distracted and doesn't look me in the eye. He tells me he is a Cognitive Behavioural Therapist, and I do not know what this means. In my mind, perhaps because of the films I have seen, I think that therapy is going to involve me lying on a sofa for an hour talking about myself, which is basically my idea of heaven – it is the closest I am ever going to get to being that film star in my old green notebook. Imagine my disappointment then when he barely looks up from his desk to ask me how I am. Almost a hundred quid an hour my mum is paying this man to not really give a shit. This is just my luck, I think – I can't get someone to take an interest in me even when he's being paid.

He hands me a questionnaire, as if I am taking part in a supermarket customer-service survey, or doing a magazine quiz. Do I strongly agree that I feel suicidal? Would I slightly disagree that I spend more time than is normal obsessing over things? Would I say that I find it moderately hard to experience enjoyment of everyday activities? Do I ever feel like hurting myself or others? Have I considered setting fire to things? I fill it out as he makes a call to his secretary about his schedule. I feel like a fraud. I am neither suicidal, murderous nor a pyromaniac. What am I doing here?

At the next session a week later, he seems to have forgotten who I am – perhaps because my mental conditions were not spectacular enough and didn't involve criminality – and spends the first twenty minutes of our hour-long meeting reading his notes as a reminder. When it's over, I tell my mother that I think she is wasting her money. The antidepressants have kicked in. I feel OK. The danger has receded, leaving me only with my phrases, which I have now uttered so often they are printed on my tongue's muscle memory. I am out of the fog. So I stop going.

If I could go back and talk to my by then eighteen-year-old self, I would say, 'No, no. You MUST keep going. If not to him, then to someone else. Find a Cognitive Behavioural Therapist who will see you for fifty quid an hour, and keep seeing them. You may feel well now, but there will be times in the future when you won't, and you will be thankful for the tools that the therapist will arm you with.' But hindsight is a wonderful thing. Mental illness isn't. Part of the cruelty of it is that while it feels like it will go on forever at the time, it can be relatively fleeting – a quick, sharp, shock that can be gone before you have had a chance to get a grip on it. And when you feel well, it is almost impossible to remember the full horror of how you felt when you weren't. It is as if it happened to another person, in another time, or some strange, parallel universe. And it will be almost twenty years before I actually find myself some proper help. Twenty bloody years – and I'm one of the lucky ones, with resources and support and some sort of guidance.

But right now I am eighteen and I do not have the benefit of hindsight. My A-level results are good – two As and a B might sound thick as pig shit now, when people routinely sit them before their fourth birthday, but at the time it was considered impressive – and I win a place at UCL to study History of Art. Again, if I could go back and talk to my eighteen-year-old self I would say, 'Don't do History of Art. No, really, don't. You think you're going to go to university and meet loads of amazing boys while discovering yourself in art galleries as you study the enlightening world of the Renaissance? (And by the way, calling it the re-nahssance doesn't make you sound sophisticated. It makes you sound like a twat.) You think that you are going to become a political revolutionary, join the Socialist Workers Party and become some arty boy's lover and muse? Well you won't. There will be only one boy on your course, and he is gay. You will live not in an ivy-covered hall, but on the eighth floor of a tower block off the Euston Road, a tower block with a broken lift and a shared bathroom with drains full of other people's hair. You hate other people's hair! Also, you won't spend that much time in art galleries. You will have about eight hours of lectures a week, which you will not be able to get used to after fourteen years of intense schooling, and you will spend the rest of the time lying in your tower block with dirty plates on your desk. And you won't even do the periods of art you are interested in. Michelangelo? Give me a break. Cezanne? You're having a laugh, love. Instead, your lecturer will show you slides of black squares that are supposedly masterpieces, and he will say to you, "This black square represents all black squares and their freedom from political ideology." And you will think, "Does it bollocks," and go back to Mummy and Daddy and announce you are dropping out, having not even stuck at it for a term, and everyone will think you're a failure . . . all before you have even turned nineteen!'

Hindsight. It's not really a wonderful thing, is it? It's actually a sarcastic little fucker.

But I am getting ahead of myself. I am always getting ahead of myself, marrying myself off to men I have only just met – or, in the case of David Duchovny, to men I have not even met – and winning top journalism prizes without ever having written an article. If my brain isn't taunting me with the possibility I might be a serial killer, it is teasing me by being 10,000 steps ahead in fantasy land. It is one of my most ludicrous traits, along with occasionally believing that I can save the world through the power of a few phrases muttered under my breath while nobody is looking. And, of course, I *know* this is ludicrous – at times I have thought of OCD as the sane person's mental illness – but I am completely powerless to stop it. Round and round the phrases go in my head – 'I'd rather I died than anyone else', 'everyone will live until they are a hundred and eight' – an internal jukebox that makes having a Rick Astley song stuck in your head seem like an absolute pleasure.

So before I go to university for ten minutes, I need to tell you about the time I realise I am losing my hair. I know, I know. Put together in a book this must all seem terribly bleak, as if my adult life is one long series of melancholic episodes, but I promise you there have been happy times, like . . . well, I can't remember them now. And you haven't come here to read about the time I had a really fun day out at Chessington World of Adventures, have you? Come on. Get real. You want the juicy stuff. You want to know about me becoming as bald as a coot.

It is a rainy Sunday the summer after I think I am a serial killer and just before I start at university. In an uncharacteristic move, a ceasefire has been called betwixt my sister and me. I think there is a thawing of relations when we both realise that I will be moving out and that we love each other, really. So that time she asked me to play Sylvanians with her, and she carefully set up her village (post office, school, shop), only for me to sit down and shout 'EARTHQUAKE!!' as I destroyed her life's work? Forgotten about. The moment I locked her in a cupboard until she knew the names of New Kids on the Block off by heart? 'It was for my own good!' she would surely say if pressed now. 'No self-respecting seven-year-old in the late eighties could go to school without being able to list Joe McIntyre, Donnie Wahlberg, Danny Wood, Jon and Jordan Knight. She was doing me a favour!' (Although now, as I write this, I am thoroughly appalled by my behaviour and not at all sure of my assertion in the previous chapter that I wouldn't hurt a fly, given that locking one's sister in a cupboard is clearly the work of a psychopath.)

Anyway, that Sunday afternoon we are having a truly wonderful time – me about to go off to university, the serial killer episode all but a distant memory; my sister about to get rid of me for good. We are watching *The Simpsons*, she is straightening my hair (why is it that when teenage girls are feeling happy, their default action is always to play with each other's hair? Is it conditioning, from a childhood spent with dollies?) and all is well with the world. It is more than well. It is great.

'Oh,' says my sister.

'Oh?' I reply.

'Oh dear,' says my sister.

Now at this point, I think it is safe to say that there are certain phrases you want to hear as the little sister you once locked in a cupboard stands behind you brandishing a flaming hot pair of hair straighteners – 'Oh what beautiful tresses you have' or 'Oh your locks are so thick'. But 'Oh dear'? Not so much.

'What's wrong?' I say, trying not to turn my head and burn myself in the process.

'Nothing,' she lies.

'Why did you say "oh dear" then?'

'Did I? I don't think I did. I think I said, "Oh dear, Scratchy has been defeated by Itchy again."'

'No you didn't. That's not what you said. Itchy and Scratchy haven't even been in this episode.'

'I was just thinking out loud about my favourite episode where Scratchy is defeated again by Itchy.'

'Well THAT'S a lie. You barely think, let alone out loud.'

'Hey, I thought we were finally friends?' says my sister, who seems genuinely hurt by my flippancy.

'I'm sorry. I was only joking. Anyway, why did you really say, "Oh dear"?'

'It's just . . .' I feel her lift up my hair at the back of my head. 'It's just, and I'm sure it's absolutely nothing, but there's a little . . . well, there's a little bald patch here.'

I immediately raise my right hand to my scalp and

run my fingers through it. Sure enough, there is a wonderfully, almost soothingly, smooth patch right in the middle of the back of my head. I rub it with my index finger and marvel at how delicate the skin there feels, like a wafer-thin membrane between my brain and the outside world. It is the size of a 50 pence coin – small, insubstantial, irrelevant.

'You're right,' I say cheerily. 'It's probably nothing. Now carry on straightening my hair, please.'

And that, as far as I am concerned, is that.

As any person lacking self-awareness and wisdom will tell you, if you ignore something, it will go away. Right? I mean, what could possibly go wrong with this fool-proof plan? History is littered with examples of problems that went away for being ignored, isn't it? Napoleon, the Nazis, and so on and so on. Doctors are forever saying, 'If you find something that seems amiss, just turn a blind eye to it because it will, in all likelihood, probably go away.' Aren't they?

But I do wonder what might have happened if I had properly been able to ignore that small hairless patch, i.e. if I had never actually noticed it in the first place, which is to say could I blame my sister for this? Just joking. Sort of. Anyway, hair loss is, of course, physical, but over the next few years, as bald patches become as normal to me as spots and blackheads, I will realise that it can also be exacerbated by the panic you experience when your finger idles over a freshly smooth piece of scalp. 'Oh God, it's happening again. This time, will my eyebrows and eyelashes and pubic hair go, too?' (The pubic hair, I guess, wouldn't be so bad, if only because it would save me having to hack away at my bikini line with a blunt razor every time I go swimming. But I digress. I always digress.) The point is, had we not found that patch that afternoon, had we decided to do something more constructive than 'play with each other's hair', like, I dunno, go to a museum, or sell home-made lemonade (ha!) to raise money for the local refuge for abandoned kittens, might the course of my history have been altered radically? Might I have gone on to not develop an eating disorder? Might the crippling insecurity have been bypassed and with it the whole hard-drinking, drug-taking, shag-anyone-who-expresses-even-the-tiniest-interest phase? And more pertinently, would I even have wanted that? You know, some of them were good shags.

There goes hindsight again, boring and preachy and trying to teach me a lesson even though, as I write this, I am thirty-five and married with a mortgage and a small child. Thank you very much, hindsight.

But back to 1998. I am eighteen, and about to go to university with a head full of hopes and dreams, and my hair is falling out. Over the next few weeks, the bald patch grows to the size of a £5 note, and then a tenner, before being joined by another patch of similar dimensions. I have no pictures of myself at the time since I could think of nothing worse than documenting my hideous physical deformity, but I do not need photographic evidence to remember with complete clarity what greeted me every time I looked in the mirror – the man from the Hamlet cigar advert, or Bobby Charlton. Pick any balding bloke with a combover, and I looked worse than he did. I looked like Donald Trump, but with less hair.

No eighteen-year-old girl should ever have to look like Donald Trump.

This, I think, is just my luck. First I think I'm dying of AIDS, then that I'm a serial killer, and now this. Give me a break, universe, give me a break! Little do I know that female hair loss can be caused by stress. But while the opportunity for self-pity is large here, and my mother later tells me that she cries at least three times a week about her balding daughter, I initially seem to take it in my stride. What else am I going to do? Lie in bed under a shroud? Lock myself away by joining a convent?

Instead, I put all my effort into hiding this strange affliction that seems to have befallen me. This, I soon realise, is futile. A gust of wind could pick up or I could get wedged under someone's armpit on the tube, and all of my hard work is undone in an instant. I buy head scarves, which are, thankfully, fashionable at the time and make me look more like Heidi than Donald Trump.

'Are you off to milk some cows?' shouts a man at me in the street one day.

'No,' snaps my sister. 'She's going to the wig shop because her hair is falling out.'

'Sorry,' says the man, looking mortified.

'Wanker,' says my sister, under her breath.

'You didn't have to do that,' I tell her, though I am thankful.

'Yes I did. What gave him the right to comment on your appearance?'

'Just one thing. If you ever find me in a wig shop, shoot me.'

'It would be my pleasure.'

At the dinner table, I offer up theories as to why my hair is falling out, forgetting that hair loss is one of the possible side effects of antidepressants.

'I wonder if it's because of that summer we went to the Isle of Wight, and I spent every day of the holiday squirting lemon juice on my hair in the hope of making it more blonde. Do you remember that?'

'Yes,' says my father. 'It rained every day and Mum didn't lock the roof rack properly on the drive back so all my clothes went flying out on to the A3.'

'I can't believe you are still going on about that,' snaps my mother. 'It was three years ago. Maybe if your father hadn't drunk so much the night before, he could have packed the roof rack himself.'

She said 'your father'. I should have known their marriage was over then.

'Excuse me,' I interrupt. 'I thought we were supposed to be talking about the fact your eighteen-year-old daughter has less hair than your seventy-five-year-old father.'

'It's always about you,' says my sister, who has managed to get to the age of sixteen without having a single funny turn.

'Anyway. It could be the lemon juice. Or perhaps the nits.'

'Yuk,' shouts my brother.

'I'd appreciate a little less lip from you given you're the reason everyone in this house has head lice the whole time. It's no wonder my hair has fallen out, given the twice-monthly shampoo with insecticide.'

I set about working out what is wrong with me. I get on the number 27 bus and head to my nearest internet café – a forty-minute journey FFS, FYI millennials – and there I use something called 'Yahoo' to search the 'world wide web' for information on female hair loss. I learn that I probably have something called 'alopecia areata', which is an autoimmune disease that causes spot baldness. I feel grateful not to have alopecia totalis, which, as you can probably tell from the name, involves complete baldness, and reflect on the fact that I am lucky my hair has not fallen out because of, say, chemotherapy.

'Basically,' I say to my mother when I get home that evening, 'the immune system rejects the hair follicle. It attacks it so it doesn't grow.'

'Why does it do that?' asks my mother, not unreasonably.

'Do I look like a doctor?'

So back we go to the brown surgery with the brown waiting room and the brown seats and the same weary-looking receptionist, and this time we are seen by a female doctor, who appears not to have slept for ten days, and looks like she is possibly considering prescribing herself some heavy pharmaceuticals.

She gives me a look that I am convinced says, 'You are bothering me with this when there are actual ill people out there sitting on the brown seats in the brown waiting room?' Then she says, 'Stress.' That's all. One word. 'Stress.' She says it over and over again, until eventually I begin to worry for her health. 'Stress, stress, stress, stress, stress.' She pauses for a moment, stands up and peers over my bald scalp. 'Or hormones.'

To this day, stress and hormones remain my least favourite causes of illness, owing to the fact there is NOTHING. YOU. CAN. DO. ABOUT. THEM. Stress? I am always stressed. I am stressed when I am not stressed because what is life if not ONE LONG HORMONE-FUELLED STRESS OUT?

86

Ahem.

She gives me a prescription for steroids, which makes the patches disappear only for them to reappear elsewhere. We go to a homeopath, who gives me tiny little pills that I immediately presume to be full of bullshit once she has told me my alopecia is probably because of all the Diet Coke I drink (I'm too gobsmacked to tell her I don't drink Diet Coke). And in the midst of all this, devoid of hair and self-esteem, I start university.

It never stands a chance, does it?

When you are eighteen and already a university drop-out with very little hair, things have a way of seeming a little bit bleak. My friends are off living the high life as freshers or gap-year students, writing letters that talk of endless drinking and shagging, while I am a thumb-sucking loser with a blankie instead of a boyfriend and a load of bald patches. This was not part of the script – the OCD, the alopecia, the failure to finish even a term of university . . . none of it, really. Had everything gone to plan, by now I would have a string of boyfriends, a despairing liver and a treatable STD that would teach me a very-important-lesson, leading me to get serious, join the student newspaper where I am eventually promoted to editor, shortly before meeting the love of my life. Instead, I face the very real possibility that I will die alone but for the cats who will eventually turn on me, too, and devour my decaying body.

Like I said – bleak.

My efforts to appear upbeat and positive about everything soon evaporate into thin air, much like the hair I used to have on my head. It's not that I feel self-pity or melancholy or misery. I just feel nothing. I am a hairless husk, a humanoid on autopilot. You could wave your hands in front of my glassy eyes and I would not take the slightest bit of notice. Everything goes in one ear, and out the other. Or more so than usual.

Spaced out, numb and most probably suffering from depression, although I am too deep in it to have the faintest clue this is what it is, I take to my bed. To be more accurate, it takes to me. I feel pinned to it, stuck in it, powerless to leave it. Some people see bed as their sanctuary. For me, it begins to feel more like solitary confinement. Problem is, I seem to be the one who has locked myself up and thrown away the key.

The strangest thing is that, despite this, entire hours and days seem to go by without me even registering them. When I was in the grips of OCD, a minute felt like an hour, but here under my increasingly dirty duvet the opposite is true. I am the lone cast member of a time-lapse movie nobody would buy tickets to, a balding creature who cannot be bothered to wash what hair she has left. I must eat and drink and go to the toilet, but I have no memory of this from the time. Who remembers eating and drinking and going to the toilet anyway? When I do go out, I feel as if I am existing in a tracing-paper version of the world that has been pulled down over the real one. Everyone else is under the tracing paper, going about their lives, and I'm on top of them, a pencil-faint line that could so easily be rubbed out.

At some point my mother is forced to make one of her interventions. She stands in the doorway, probably looking cross although everything is a bit hazy as I haven't put my contact lenses in for something like six days now. Hazy, and smelly, on account of the fact I can't even be bothered to shower.

'You can't spend the rest of your life in bed,' she says.

'Who says so?'

'I just did.'

'What's wrong with spending the rest of your life in bed, anyway? It's what everyone secretly wants, isn't it? For life to be one long lie-in. In many ways, I'm living the dream. You're just jealous.'

'You'll get bed sores if you stay there much longer, you know.'

'What's a few bed sores when I look like me, anyway?'

'Bryony, please.'

I feel sorry for my mother now. I had no idea at the time that her marriage to my father was ending, and on top of that she had to deal with a depressed eighteen-year-old daughter who looked like Donald Trump. I mean, this is the kind of thing you wouldn't wish on your worst enemy, isn't it, and yet there I was, all 'yeah-whatevs-shut-up-I-hate-you', with no apparent interest in helping myself let alone anybody close to me. If a year ago I had been chanting to keep my family safe, now my behaviour suggested I held them in disdain. I could slap eighteen-year-old Donald Trump me, really I could.

I turn my back on her and tell her to go away, but I can feel her icy stare piercing into my back.

'MUM, just LEAVE ME ALONE!' I huff and that is it, that is all she can stand.

'ENOUGH is ENOUGH!' she bellows, as I feel her sit down on the bed. 'At least have the decency to look at me,' and I can hear the heartbreaking sound of desperation in her voice. I turn round with a grimace on my face, not quite ready to show her that I am softening. 'I know you've had a hard time. I know that your A-levels weren't the easiest ride and that the alopecia has been horrible. But that's no reason to shut yourself away from us. We are not the enemy. We have supported you through the decision to drop out of university, and you seem completely unaware of it. You have no idea that locked away in this room in your own misery, you are dictating the mood of the rest of the house. Your sister is upset by it, your little brother

doesn't know what to think, and your father and I . . .'
Later, I will play this conversation back and wonder if
I had anything to do with what happened to them.
'Your father and I are obviously really distressed by
your behaviour.'

'MY BEHAVIOUR?' I storm, several months of held-
back self-pity exploding at once. 'YOU'RE distressed?
Why are you making this ALL ABOUT YOU?'

My mother looks at me with quiet fury. 'Because,
Bryony Gordon, you need to learn that it isn't always
about *you*.'

And at that, she leaves the room.

Well, that certainly shocks me out of my stupor, I can
tell you. I lie there prickling with her anger and the
realisation that being a self-indulgent so-and-so is not
going to get me anywhere. It is going to get me nowhere
very, very slowly. And Mum is right. I can't spend the
rest of my life in bed, because not only will I get bed
sores but my muscles are also bound to waste away,
which, when you add in the alopecia, is not exactly a
good look.

So I go downstairs. The look on my mother's face
when I tip-toe into the kitchen suggests that this is
something of a surprise.

'Hello,' I say, quietly.

My sister looks up from her homework. My brother
briefly stops drawing on the wall.

'Hello,' says my mother. 'How nice of you to come down and join us.'

'I thought I should probably try and stop making it all about me.' The faintest hint of a smile appears on my face. My mum comes over and cuddles me, and it feels good, really good.

We decide that I should try to get a job while I work out what to do next. 'There's a kid's shop on the high street advertising for help,' says my dad, so I head back to the internet café forty minutes away, work out how to create a CV, and try not to feel too disconsolate about how threadbare mine is going to appear, given my lack of experience, professional or otherwise.

'You could put that you babysit,' says my mother, grasping at ever-decreasing straws, 'which means you have ample experience with young children.'

I spend an hour and a half 'styling' my hair, or what is left of it, in preparation for dropping off my CV at the shop. This involves me washing it in such a heightened state of anxiety you would be forgiven for thinking, were you perverted enough to be watching me in the shower, that a troop of deadly tarantulas had just marched up the drain. Every rub of the scalp feels as if it has the potential to leave me completely bald. Every strand of hair in the plughole feels like a tiny defeat. Then comes the 'blow dry', a sight so pathetic it is almost laughable – watching someone with alopecia dry her follicles is like watching a tiny, hairless dog get towelled down after a bath – and finally, the tempting and teasing of thin, lank strands over shiny, pink head, all fixed down with grips that have nothing to grip on to.

I put on mascara, because I at least have a half decent face, now horribly exposed by the departure of all the hair I used to hide behind. Blusher and lipstick, too. I have spent hours considering my outfit so that it looks 'effortlessly stylish', as my magazines say. (Oh God, the effort we must put into looking effortlessly stylish!) A pair of jeans, some ankle boots, a T-shirt and a blazer.

I realise it has been months since I last cared what I looked like.

It's a cold but bright day, a sharp day, so I borrow a scarf my sister has from the brand's grown-up range, and put on the matching gloves. 'You look great,' says my mum, waving me out the door, being careful not to ruffle my hair and undo all my hard work, and I feel positive, I feel happy. The wind is stronger than I had realised from within the confines of my warm, cosy, home, so I pick up my pace, acutely aware of the potential for things to go horribly wrong.

I walk into the shop and am grateful for the warm blast of air from the heating over the entrance. A small child stares at me as I stand in the entrance, his mother pulling him away with an embarrassed look on her face, but I am enjoying the warmth too much to put two and two together. So with wind-stung cheeks and a deep breath, I approach the cash registers and ask a girl who is even younger than I am if I could talk to the manager about the jobs going. She nods silently and tells me to wait where I am, before disappearing to find her boss.

The woman who returns seems terribly grown-up, although with my old friend hindsight, I realise she is probably no more than twenty-two. I smile at her, pull out my CV, and start to speak, but she doesn't appear to be listening. Her eyes dart up to my scalp, and then, as if realising she has been caught, which she has, back down to my eyes. She looks at me squarely, smiles the most insincere of smiles, and cuts me off mid-sentence.

'Thank you for your interest,' she says. 'But I'm afraid we have filled the last position.'

The young shop girl reappears at the till, looking uncomfortable.

'Oh,' I say, trying to gather my composure. 'I'm terribly sorry. I saw the sign in your window and thought you were still looking.'

'It's nothing personal, of course,' continues the manager, which naturally tells me she is about to say something highly personal. 'Even if we did have jobs available, I'm not sure you'd like it here. You don't really have the right look for us. I'd love to give you a chance, but sadly, I have to think about the company's image. I'm sure you understand.'

And the worst thing is that I do understand. I understand so much that I feel ashamed and stupid for ever having hoped to have a job folding up jumpers. Had this happened ten years later, I might have been able to sue her for discrimination, or shame her in a Facebook post that would then go viral, but this is before the onset of political correctness or the concept of equality or what you look like on the outside not counting for a bean. So instead I do the only thing I can think of, which is mumble, 'I understand,' before turning on my heel and getting the hell out of there. It's pathetic, I know, but I am beaten down by my alopecia, on the tail end of a depression, and I am fed up with feeling ashamed. I am fed up and very, very angry. I get home, and I run up to my bedroom, and I think, 'Fuck that woman and fuck that company and fuck their fucking image.' I'm going to catch a break, I tell myself. I'm going to catch the biggest fucking break, and nobody is going to stop me – least of all myself.

5

I think I might be fat

My body had never felt like mine, not really. I realise that now, with age and lines and fat and the tiniest bit of wisdom. Does any young woman feel as if her body is hers, anyway? The cat-calling, the leering, the sense sometimes that your only purpose is to be pleasing to the men you pass in the street or stand next to at a bar, the feeling that you are a cow at market, bred only to be useful to someone else – this was what it often felt like when I was coming of age. And it is what it still occasionally feels like even now, when I receive emails and Tweets from men who have seen my picture in the paper, telling me that I am fat and disgusting and that they'd never sleep with me – as if I was queuing up to have sex with them in the first place.

Even before my hair had started to fall out, my body did things I did not want it to. You know, obviously, about my brain's ability to make me think I was dying or that I might hurt people, but there were other betrayals, too. At eleven I grew breasts the size of children's party balloons and by thirteen I had become accustomed to walking with my head down to avoid the lingering stares of men old enough to know better. By fifteen it was so normal for friends to make jokes about my boobs that I had started making them myself – I was Bryony, a walking, talking pair of tits.

My eyesight failed me, my appendix had to be ripped out, and soon after that I found I couldn't breathe. If inhaling and exhaling feels a bit like going up one side of a mountain and coming down the other, why did I keep falling down the same side, unable to reach the peak or fill my lungs with oxygen? At the time the doctor thought it was probably just a case of childhood asthma that I would grow out of, prescribing an inhaler that made me feel woozy with gratitude. I now recognise the sensation for what it was, and what, occasionally, it still is – blind panic. Anxiety. My brain taking control of my body again, without any apparent input from me. It always amazes me how the very systems charged with keeping us going seem to turn on us with such ease.

But weirdly, the encounter with the woman in the shop gives me renewed focus. I am almost thankful for her blind prejudice, because it is the short, sharp shock I need to take back control of my body and of my life. I had swiped my mother's address book while in the process of dropping out of university, writing to several of her contacts asking for work experience, and by chance, having sent out twenty letters without a single reply, I now get one. I see this as a sign, an almighty signal from above that me and journalism are meant to be! No matter that my mother has probably begged, pleaded and borrowed to get this letter to me. I am too desperate for something good to happen to notice, and if this makes me guilty of nepotism, I do not give a damn. It is what I want to do, and I am completely, manically, determined to do it.

My two-week internship is on the *Sunday Express*, where, upon arrival, I quickly realise why they are in need of a work-experience person. They have just six staff, including the editor. Had I had any modicum of sense, I would have seen this as the warning for newspapers that it so clearly was, the ominous sign of what was to follow everywhere else, with budgets slashed and readerships in decline and redundancies on the cards, so much so that the only person they could afford to recruit was an almost-nineteen-year-old with no hair or self-esteem . . . but I don't have any modicum of sense. I just think it's great.

Here, my alopecia isn't a problem. In fact, it's a story. 'You should totally write 800 words about it for the weekend,' barks the editor in my first week, which I do, even having my picture taken to accompany it. I remember this well, for all the wrong reasons. The photographer, a chap in his mid-forties who is also losing his hair, makes me stand with my hands on my hips before telling me to lick my lips, as this will give me a 'natural' smile. Reader, I believe him – until I inform my mother about this nifty trick and she tells me that if he ever tries this again, I am to kick him in the balls to bring about a 'natural' wince.

I make friends with John, the features lackey, who takes me to the pub and gives me assignments he does not want to do. These involve:

• Dressing up as Chewbacca for a feature on *Star Wars* memorabilia. 'Be thankful that you didn't have to be Jabba the Hutt like last week's workie,' says John, as he hands me the itchy costume. Despite this humiliation, I feel useful and content in the outfit, which, I tell myself, is the most hair I have had on my body for some time. I even manage to crack a 'Chewie, we're home!' gag, which impresses John, if nobody else.

• Being placed in a giant, inflatable ball and rolled down a hill for a photograph to accompany an article he has done on a new trend called zorbing, which has the effect of bringing back the childhood asthma I thought I had grown out of. 'I think you're having a panic attack!' says the instructor, who pulls me out of the giant, inflatable ball, gasping for air, but even then I do not click.

• Going to Boots to buy tights for the editor after hers have laddered.

• Being sent in a cab to a restaurant where the editor is having a long lunch, to give her a copy of the *Evening Standard* because it features some exciting breaking news about a politician being sacked. This, I realised when Twitter and Facebook came into existence, bringing with them news at the touch of a button, is why people refer to newspapers as the 'dead-tree media'.

The fortnight passes in a blur, and they ask me if I want to stay on for another fortnight, and another after that, and before long John is promoted from lackey to senior lackey, and I am offered his job. I start writing regularly about yoof issues, even earning as much as £125 a week, and when I hear through the grapevine about a writing job going on the teenage section of the *Daily Telegraph*, I do something completely bonkers and apply. Even more bonkers is the fact that I get the job. I am nineteen, and a writer on a national news-paper, even if all it involves is penning 200-word pieces about Tina from S Club 7's favourite colour.

Fuck you, woman in the shop! Fuck you OCD! Fuck you alopecia! I'm finally making something of myself.

But . . . well, in life, as I am finding out, there's always a but, isn't there?

I throw up for the first time soon after I start my job at the *Telegraph*, and shortly before my parents announce their intention to divorce, which isn't that surprising given they have barely spoken to each other for . . . what? A year? Two? The sound of nothing more than the kitchen clock ticking has become so normal I have barely even noticed it. Tick-tock, tick-tock, it goes, as the marriage of my parents silently disintegrates. It has happened so slowly but surely that by the time my father spills the beans one Sunday afternoon I am, of course, bristling with anger, but entirely expected anger.

It is anger that has been stored up and ready to go for some time. I do not see a link between the breakdown of my family and the start of my bulimia. I just try to see it as an inconvenience, because I am a grown-up, and grown-ups are not supposed to boo hoo about their mummy and daddy splitting up. It is unbecoming and not terribly dignified. Of course, now I can see that having the rug pulled out from under you and your staunch belief that your parents are in a perfectly functioning dysfunctional relationship might have had something to do with me developing an eating disorder (that and the fact that the most frequent mental condition to co-exist in people with eating disorders is obsessive compulsive disorder). But back then, I am convinced the divorce is nothing more than a little bit irritating. It's so predictable that this would happen now, when everything seems to be going so swimmingly. It is so predictable that life should deliver one of its buts just as I'm about to interview Westlife for the first time.

'We've been trying to shield you from it while you were doing so well,' my mother tells me later when we sit down to discuss the only plans she has made with my father for eons and eons. 'We told your sister and your brother a while ago because we thought they should know.'

I mean, she told an eleven-year-old child before she plucked up the courage to tell me.

But the thing is, I *am* doing well. I really am. I may be sneaking upstairs to throw up my dinner every night, but they don't know that, and anyway, in my mind, the ritual purging of anything I eat is only a sign of how well I am doing. I have a job I love, a wage that allows me to shop freely at Topshop, and now I am finally gaining some power over the body that has let me down for so long.

Although I am not fat at this point, not by any stretch of the imagination, I have always mistakenly believed I am. For young women, fat is more often than not a mental state rather than a physical one. It's the place we go in our heads whenever we dare to think we might look good. 'Let me admire myself in this new Topshop dr— . . . OH-MY-GOD-LOOK-HOW-FAT-I-AM-IN-IT. LOOK-AT-MY-BUM-AND-MY-BINGO-WINGS-AND-JESUS-

FUCKING-CHRIST-JUST-BY-BUYING-THIS-
DRESS-I-SEEM-TO-HAVE-DEVELOPED-THE-
THIGHS-OF-AN-ENGLAND-RUGBY-PLAYER.'

'You look gorgeous in it,' comforts a friend.

'IT'S-HIDEOUS! WHAT-WAS-I-THINKING?
I-HAVE-AN-EXPENSIVE-EDUCATION-AND-
READ-NEWSPAPERS-AND-YET-I-HAVE-BEEN-
RENDERED-A-COMPLETE-FOOL-BY-THIS-
PIECE-OF-MATERIAL-THAT-I-ACTUALLY-PAID-
£40-FOR!'

And so on and so on.

Eating disorders, such as anorexia, bulimia and binge-
eating, affect more than 725,000 people in the UK
(according to the most recent and robust data commissioned by the charity Beat and released in 2015). But
disordered eating seems to be far more prevalent. It
seemed to be the norm when I was growing up. While
our parents were careful to feed us balanced diets, they
were busy starving themselves. It's the same today, only
this disordered eating is, terrifyingly, dressed up as
healthy eating – it's treats such as kale shakes and
chocolate cake that's actually made of avocado; it's
some chia seeds followed by a bit of seaweed. They
call this orthorexia, and its rise to prominence is thanks
to young, beautiful bloggers with barely a nutritional
qualification between them. It's like putting the luna-
tics in charge of the asylum.

As the mother of a young girl, I fear this world

where it has become completely normal to upload to the internet pictures of yourself and your body that have first gone through several filters. I fear this world where the body seems to rule at the expense of the mind. I don't know how I would have survived it as a teenager, and I worry about how my daughter will navigate her way through it. So I try hard not to talk about weight or criticise the way I look every second moment of the day. I try hard to appear normal, but it's difficult. It's difficult because this body shit is basically engrained in us; it's part of our DNA. Every woman I ever came across as a child feared being ginormous and I'm guessing every woman they ever came across as children feared being ginormous – it just appeared to be a female's default setting. This isn't to say I blame my mother for my eating disorder; nor do I point the finger of blame at women's magazines or fashion models. That would be far too easy, not to mention lazy, too. It's just to say that if you are a young woman in a vaguely confused state and a slightly difficult place, trying to regain some control over the madness in your head, the outward appearance of your body can seem as good a place as any to start.

And start I do. My focus on my work is matched only by my focus on losing weight, on my clavicle becoming more pronounced and my cheekbones becoming edgier and edgier. I have a vigour that borders on the manic and seems to be completely in tune with my all-or-nothing character. (To this day, I would still rather have no drink whatsoever than just one drink. I'll have either a salad or four portions of pasta. I'm no psychologist but I'm guessing this compulsive behaviour is something quite common in people with OCD.)

I go through the working day without putting anything more than two litres of water, five cans of Diet Coke (what *would* the homeopath have said?) and a packet of Marlboro Lights in my mouth. I live off caffeine, nicotine and adrenaline. Hunger pangs, once uncomfortable, now become strangely pleasant reminders that my body is in the process of devouring itself.

Now, such a diet, if you could even call it that, would cause me to collapse in a gibbering, weeping heap, begging for carbohydrates and my bed. But aged nineteen, I do not feel so much as faint. In fact, I feel great. I feel invincible.

At night, when I get home, I eat my dinner carefully, in food groups – vegetables first, then protein, then carbohydrates if I am feeling particularly gluttonous. This is so that when I come to throw it all up, I will know when I have completely emptied my stomach by the sight of some masticated vegetables in the toilet bowl. Never has someone been so glad of the sight of regurgitated broccoli, let me tell you.

Once I have finished dinner, I wait five minutes or

so and make small talk – 'nice weather we are having', 'how is the divorce going?' et cetera et cetera – before excusing myself to go upstairs to my room. It is very important I make small talk for no longer than ten minutes, because I have read that after this the calories have a way of sticking around.

Reader, please do not be as stupid as I was and see this as some sort of guide.

Upstairs, I put on the music of whatever shite turn-of-the-millennium band I happen to be into at the time – 5ive, Blue, please shoot me now – turn up the volume loud (as if my family didn't have enough on their plates) and then go and run a bath. Running a bath is a tactic I employ to help drown out the sound of my retching. While the taps are on I glug back some water, which seems to help with the ease of vomit, wet my right index finger, which seems to make shoving it down my throat a bit more bearable, and then I fling my head over the toilet bowl and off I go, vomit, vomit, vomit, while downstairs everyone plays at being a not-so-happy family.

Some people find sick repulsive and, granted, I have never been fond of spotting someone else's. But my own doesn't bother me. In fact, I come to feel quite affectionate towards it. It is therapeutic, cleansing, even. The more sick I have in the toilet bowl, on my face and up my nostrils (did you know that sick also comes out of your nostrils? Take my word for it, it does), the more that my eyes water and get bloodshot from it, the better. I'm not for one minute trying to sell this behaviour to you – quite the opposite. I'm just trying to explain to you the twisted (well, sick) logic behind it.

I invest heavily in mouthwash, mints and dental floss. The smell of my perfume, made by Clinique and ironically called Happy, hangs heavily in the air in an attempt to mask the toxic smell of vomit.

I am doing well. I am doing well. But even if I'm not, everybody is too wrapped up in their own issues to notice.

Back then, that is just how I like things to be.

Moving out of home for the first time – the first proper time after my false start with university – is meant to be exciting for any number of reasons, isn't it? The chance to bring boys back for all-night shagging, the opportunity to have friends round and drink heavily without anyone telling you to go to bed (well, without anyone from your family telling you to go bed), the ability to decorate your room entirely in fairy lights without your mother complaining that they are a tad too 'garish'.

But for me . . . well, for me it is exciting because I will have the chance to throw up to my heart's content without any fear of being found out or flooding the bathroom because I have left the taps running and am too embroiled in vomiting up all my food to notice. My excessive bathroom use is becoming an elephant in the room, even if all the voices in my head insist that this title actually belongs to me. And so it is that I am quite militant about moving out. My mother tells me I don't have to. Weirdly, she almost begs me to stay, as if she is now so lonely that spending time with an obsessive-compulsive lunatic is preferable to the alternative. But with a fully fledged eating disorder and a career under way I am insistent on 'getting my own place' (which I always say with a not-very-grown-up huff).

Of course, the process of 'getting my own place' is not quite as simple as I had been led to believe from programmes such as *Friends*, where glossy twenty-somethings miraculously find themselves living in Manhattan loft apartments, or *This Life*, where insanely hot and interesting twenty-somethings miraculously find themselves living in shared houses with other insanely hot and interesting twenty-somethings. Finding a place to live on the internet is still seen as only marginally safer than visiting the wing that houses sex offenders at your local prison. Estate agents have a habit of showing you properties you could never afford, or ones that you could afford but would never want to live in. So I am left leafing through the pages of *Loot*, a depressing paper full of classified ads that ask for 'no jobseekers', which ironically makes me feel as if I am one, a vagabond scraping the barrel of London's housing market for somewhere to throw up safely and with impunity. (I decide not to include this as one of my requirements when speaking to the few estate agents I do call up. 'I'm looking for a one-bedroom place with plumbing good enough to handle the, ahem, excesses of a bulimic!' 'Well, Miss Gordon, we have just the property for you . . .')

The flat I eventually find is in east London – trendy, trendy, grown-up east London! – above a chicken shop and an outlet called 'The Ashtray' that specialises in smoking equipment. This seems a somewhat apt place to be. The flat is actually a bedsit that happens to have its own bathroom, or 'wet room', as the landlord loftily calls it – a shower perilously close to the loo and sink, the likes of which I only ever encounter again on a work trip to China. No matter. A wet room is good enough for me and my bulimia. There is barely any kitchen to speak of, although obviously this bothers me not one jot, and the bed is actually a sofa, but it is mine; or sort of mine, given that I am only renting it.

Away from prying eyes and ears and curious yet queasy noses, my bulimia reaches new levels of disgusting. I celebrate moving into my own place with a huge takeaway from McDonald's, which I promptly throw up. It amazes me what I can shove into my body. Two or three burgers at a time, not to mention fries and chicken nuggets. It seems so nifty to me that I have found a way to eat what I want without ever gaining a pound. Like magic, almost. I am cheating the system and getting away with it. And I am too impressed with my cunning to realise that rather than controlling my body, I am punishing it. I have no idea that the vomit is slowly wearing away the enamel on my teeth. I am too used to my reflection in the mirror to notice that my skin has turned sallow, or that the capillaries under my cheeks are breaking.

Here in this place of my own the binge and purge mentality of bulimia really runs wild. If I starve myself all week, I can spend all weekend eating yards of pizza. I can eat scotch eggs by the dozen, pork pies by the score. Pints of ice cream are swallowed whole without giving myself a chance to even catch my breath. I can lose my mind in food. Entire hours can pass by without me noticing them doing so. I go numb when I binge. I float contentedly on a cloud of calories. Then I bring myself back to earth with a purge. I clear myself out. I am sharp, angular, ready, high as a kite on sugar and vomit and self-loathing.

These are the cyclical actions of an addict, but it seems ridiculous to compare bulimia to, say, heroin or alcohol addiction. And yet I surround myself with all the accoutrements of addiction – toilet plunger, for when the loo gets blocked, which is frequently; Marigolds for the same reason; endless bottles of bleach;

umpteen toothbrushes, which I use sometimes five, six, seven times a day; boxes and boxes of mints; packets and packets of chewing gum.

But it's not enough. It never is. I start to wish I could lose more weight, and more quickly. It occurs to me that bulimia is just a lazy girl's disorder, a greedy girl's disorder. Were I truly serious about getting skinny, I would be able to commit to the endless emptiness of anorexia. But I can't, no matter how hard I try. I can't deal with the loudness of the voices in my head when I don't eat anything at all – I like the slightly numb feeling I get by eating myself into a stupor. So instead I buy laxatives, meaning the food comes out of both ends. I am disgusting, ridiculous. I have actually managed to beat myself up for not having a better eating disorder; I actually think that shitting myself is the way forward.

It's easy for me to paint a grim picture of my first years as an adult. But it isn't the whole picture. Yes, I am bulimic. Yes, I am still without a full head of hair. Yes, I still have to say phrases to keep my family safe. But I am also having a good time. This isn't a popular thing to say, because in the binary world we live in, you are either happy or sad and never the twain shall meet. But while I clearly dislike myself enough to shove my fingers down my throat routinely, and while I am still ruled by obsessions and compulsions, I am also managing to have fun. I am being paid to write – and about entertaining things, like nu-metal and Craig David and totally cute bracelets to buy when out shopping with your friends.

I make new, exciting friends at work, who are a little bit older than I am and, as a result, completely awe-inspiring. Yes, I am apparently an adult but I still seem to suffer from the schoolgirl syndrome of immediately thinking the people in the years above you are cool, even if they happen to be absolute twonks. There's James, my first proper gay friend, who constantly tells me I am fabulous, and Steve, a journalist who is a bit like my older brother (and no, this is not code for 'I've met this great bloke who for years I will only view as a friend until – BOOM! – a thunderbolt moment causes us to realise we couldn't see what was right before our very eyes, and we fall in love and live happily ever after.' I need to tell you now, this is *not* that kind of book.) But mostly, there is Chloe. Chloe, a dazzling dolly mixture of a human being who looks like she should be on the cover of a Roxy Music album, not that I am in any way cool enough to know what or who Roxy Music really is. Chloe, who wears sequinned skirts to the office, teamed with a nonchalant attitude. Chloe, who apparently grew up in Belfast but moved to London at seventeen, wiping any trace of an accent in the process (that's how cool Chloe is). Chloe, who lives with her 'music executive' boyfriend in an 'apartment', not a flat, and certainly not a bedsit. Chloe, who comes out with pithy lines like 'today I'm wearing a hair-don't' and 'is there no beginning to your talents?'

Chloe, she is everything.

Together we go to showbiz parties and drink cocktails. We flirt and we dance and we get a cheap thrill out of rubbing shoulders with Z-list celebrities. We spend every evening in Soho, if not at parties then at pubs and members clubs, drinking hard and occasionally dabbling in drugs, meeting people whose faces and names and stories we will have no memory of in the morning.

Years later, when my bulimia has boiled down to once-a-week extreme binges, I will go on a date with a wild vegetarian. (He is wild not because he is a vegetarian, you understand, but because afterwards he invites me to a sex party. But that's another story altogether.) On my way home, starving, I bite into a burger and half of a back molar will fall out. It feels like one of those dreams you have where your mouth crumbles without any warning and you are completely powerless to stop it. A crack reverberates through my head, I taste metal and feel grit, and then, in shock, I place my right hand in my mouth as if this might somehow stop what is happening, might make the grit re-form into a coherent mass that can then be stuck back into the space that now exists in my gum. But it is too late, it is done. I spit the contents of my mouth into my hands – bits of tooth in a not too pleasant mix of mincemeat, lettuce, onion, ketchup and blood.

Nice. Real nice.

I have not visited a dentist since living with my parents because . . . well, why the hell would I? Dentists cost money and so do dresses and shoes and make-up. Now tell me, if you were a twenty-something, what would you prefer to buy with what little hard-earned cash you have? But now my hand is forced. Or my mouth, if you will. Too embarrassed to tell my mother, who will probably think, incorrectly, that my tooth loss is because of crack-cocaine addiction (she read about this once in the *Daily Mail*), I go to the Yellow Pages to search for a nearby dentist.

Yes, I lived as an adult in a time when we still had the Yellow Pages.

The dentist I choose is situated above a 'Cashino' (see what they did there?), which must be one of the most singularly depressing places on a high street. A mecca for deluded addicts, it's dressed up in flashing lights and year-round tinsel, as if it's going to make all your Christmasses come early and not just rob you of what little money and self-esteem you have left. As I have clearly *not* learnt from the bedsit above The Ashtray, nothing good ever comes from places situated above seedy establishments. So I climb the stairs and make myself uncomfortable in the waiting room, which is actually a hall containing two chairs and not a single magazine, not even one that happens to be five years old.

The dentist appears. He is tall, dark and angry looking. 'Breeeeeeyoknee-Grodon,' he shouts, although I have no idea why because I am the only person in the room. 'You come with me,' he snaps. Reluctantly, I do as I am told, and follow him into what I suppose I should describe as his 'office' – a room containing a threadbare dentist's chair and a phalanx of frightening equipment that looks even more scary given it is about to be wielded by a cross man who seems to barely speak any English. I move towards the chair nervously, and start to make small talk. I am paying a man who clearly couldn't give a toss about me to yank out what remains of my back molar, and I still feel the need to be polite. (This is a good analogy for most of the relationships with men I will have in my twenties.)

'Where are you from originally?' I say, an awkward smile on my face.

'Iran,' he spits.

'That's nice,' I say.

'No, not really. No human rights. Lots of executions.' He makes a throat-slitting gesture just in case I don't get it. 'It not nice, which is why I find myself here.' He gives a disconsolate shrug and sarcastically flourishes his arms around his office.

115

Sometimes, I think, sometimes I don't know I am even born.

Small talk out of the way, he begins to root around in my mouth.

'Ah, I see,' he says. 'Your tooth, it been destroyed by acid. You sick a lot? I see this in girls who sick a lot.' Luckily, his hand is in my mouth so I cannot reply.

He gets his drill out, removes what remains of my tooth, charges me a quite reasonable £60, and then asks if I want him to put in an implant, which, he adds, is £400. I thank him for his kind offer but given that £400 is a lot of money and nobody can see my missing tooth, I decide against it. And then I leave, with some cotton wool stuffed in my mouth and instructions not to smoke or drink alcohol lest I get a painful dental condition known as 'dry socket' (no laughing at the back), which occurs as a result of the exposure of infectious agents to recent scar tissue.

Well of course I get dry socket. Another trip to the Iranian, another sixty quid plus a course of antibiotics and a rueful, 'I told you so. You young British girls, you never learn. You never listen.'

And he is right. Obviously he is right. You would think that losing a tooth might shake me out of my vomit-induced stupor but I am afraid it takes a lot more than that. My tongue learns to avoid the gap in the back of my mouth, the reminder of the damage that bulimia can do. I carry on being sick, because my mind is focused on a future that only ever extends to next week.

What did I think being thin, or thinn*er*, would do? Would it make me happy, bring me a kind man, deliver me from evil? Was it the answer to all my problems, or the cause of them, or merely just a symptom of them? Did I realise that, with bulimia, I was taking a perfectly good body and making it worse? Did I know that I was snowballing from one mental-health issue to another, burying problems under yet more problems until I could barely decipher between them?

There goes hindsight again, the smart arse.

Earlier I described obsessive compulsive disorder as a disconnect between your brain and your eyes, your grey matter refusing to acknowledge what is right in front of you. Bulimia works on the same premise, I suppose, because what pains me now is that I have no idea of how good I look, how lithe my limbs are, how my stomach is in fact a gorgeous wonder to behold. I am at my perkiest and my loveliest. Bald patch or no bald patch, I am as beautiful physically as I ever will be. Mentally, I have a long, long way to go.

6

I think I might be in love

By the age of twenty I have a job, an eating disorder, and an auto-immune condition that just won't quit, but there is still one thing I haven't achieved, and that is this – I haven't fallen in love. Curiously, given my cripplingly low self-esteem and my love of vomit coupled with my lack of hair, I have yet to find a man who wants to share my special journey with me. I have yet to meet someone who finds this proposition attractive. I just can't see the dating advert, can you – or the Tinder profile, as I should probably say? Relaxed, attractive man WLTM slightly screwed-up bulimic who has had everything handed to her on a plate by her middle-class parents and yet still can't quite get her act together. These just aren't the things that someone puts down on their list of attractive qualities when searching for Mrs Right, and if they are, you probably don't want to date him. Take it from me, you really don't. Because I did date him. I dated him so you didn't have to.

Back then, I would have dated anyone so you wouldn't have to.

His name was Paul. Actually, that wasn't his name at all, but I can't tell you his real one for a number of reasons. Firstly, in the fifteen years since I first knew him, he may have grown into a decent human being who deserves his privacy. Secondly, he may not have. If that's the case, then I definitely don't want to name him, because he might fly into one of his rages, hunt me down and . . . well, I'm not quite sure what. I was never quite sure what with Paul.

I'm making him sound awful but he wasn't really. The sad truth is that people like him – bloodsuckers, vampire-boyfriends, wife-beaters – have to have some really redeeming features in order to get away with their otherwise piss-poor behaviour. They have to draw you in with something, be it charm, good looks, a cracking sense of humour or, as in Paul's case, all three. (Paul was gorgeous. Paul was hilarious. Paul almost actually glittered – until, of course, he didn't.) These things are their foils, their cover. They are what make men like him so very appealing yet dangerous. The question we often ask of people in abusive relationships is, 'Why doesn't she just leave?' And this is why

119

– because she can't. Because she's stuck in his beautiful, glistening web.

We met at one of the parties I was invited to for work. He was in PR, and was part of the team that had organised the event, a cocktail evening to celebrate the release of a DVD, or something else equally vapid. He was charming from the offset, charming and exceedingly handsome, in a classic, tall, dark way. I thought he looked like Robbie Williams, which obviously thrilled me, although I later discovered his pedigree was far better than the one belonging to my teenage crush of yesteryear. Paul had exotic ancestry, spoke several languages, had a first class degree and was biding his time in a job he clearly thought was below him – a job I wholeheartedly agreed was below him. To me, everything and everyone was below Paul, from the Queen to the Pope to the man in the moon.

He was twenty-five. This was grown-up, this was big, and I couldn't believe that he wanted to talk to little old me that night, of all the girls in the room. There were glamorous ones, confident ones, cool ones, and yet he chose to attach himself to the shy, retiring, mousy one standing in the corner (yes, I was once all of these things). Of course, I now know that these are exactly the qualities a man like Paul is drawn to. Had I been glamorous or confident or cool he wouldn't have been interested for a moment because a glamorous or confident or cool woman would have soon exposed him, found him out for what he really was and told him to sling his hook. But back then I was just flattered. Completely and utterly, overwhelmingly flattered. Not to mention thankful. Oh God, I was thankful. That night, when he asked for my number and suggested we meet up just the two of us, I could have burst with disbelief, but mostly gratitude. It came off me in waves. I may have got the bus home but in my head I actually floated there. I remember very clearly calling my mum even though I knew she would probably be in bed, and, forever getting ahead of myself, saying to her, 'I've met the man of my dreams and I can't believe my luck!'

To which she replied, 'It has nothing to do with luck, darling.'

And she was more right than she could ever have known. The truth is, I was actually unlucky with Paul, although discussing our relationship in terms of chance seems to me a little unhelpful, not to mention inaccurate. Often, in the two years that followed, I would feel that Paul and I were fated to be together, like some troubled, star-crossed lovers, but we weren't. I could have walked away the moment his red mist descended, could have chosen a different path to wander down. As I've got older I've realised that you're the master of your own fate, you make your own luck, and in the weeks that followed my first meeting with Paul I certainly made mine. I knew something wasn't quite right. I saw that the tantrums were not normal, but my brain, doing what it seemed to do best, just chose to misinterpret those initial signals and wrongly translate them as signs of positive, emotional intensity. I told myself that Paul was just passionate; this was what happened when you were in love. I told myself this because as soon as he had asked for my number I had written our future in my head – the holidays we would go on, the flat we would live in, the evenings out at the theatre we would enjoy – and I couldn't bear to let myself down. I had to grab this chance with Paul because it was entirely possible I would never have a chance with anyone as attractive as him ever again, and because I needed someone to find me attractive. I needed to feel validated physically after months and months and months and maybe even years of feeling so wrong. In short, I needed Paul for what he had come to represent in my head rather than for anything he actually was. And so, in many ways, I was entirely complicit in what was to happen next.

The first time Paul lost his temper in front of me was on our third date. Our third date, incidentally, was only three days after we had initially met, such is the speed and intensity of a hot-headed maniac (and I include myself in this description). He had texted me shortly after my call to my mum, asking if I fancied a hair of the dog the next evening, and so I had met him for a pint that turned into five pints and a snog. 'Cinema?' he had asked, shortly before placing me in a cab in a gentlemanly fashion, and I was so taken with this turn of events that of course I didn't catch myself and urge caution. Of course I didn't at any point try to play it cool. We went to see a Brazilian film with subtitles – his choice, of course – which I obviously saw as proof of his intellectual and emotional depth, and at the end of that he had said, 'OK, I don't normally take things this quickly with a girl, but how about dinner tomorrow night?' which obviously made me feel special in a way I had never done before. It made me feel like a freakin' Victoria's Secret model. Or an Ann Summers one, at the very least.

We didn't go for dinner in the end. I don't think we ever did, actually. Dinner would only have got in the way of drinking. He came to meet me near the *Telegraph*'s offices, which were then in Canary Wharf. This made me feel impossibly grown-up, as if I were starring in some superannuated movie version of my life. I could not quite believe that I had both a job and a date, and on the very same day at that.

It was springtime, and my mood seemed to match the weather – warmer, brighter, full of hope for the summer to come. I felt the giddy excitement I had only ever experienced before at a Take That concert, but this was different. This was ridiculously real. I had started the week alone, insecure, unsure, but I seemed to be ending it actually dating someone. I had to pinch myself to check I wasn't dreaming, to check I hadn't accidentally fallen through the space-time continuum into some parallel universe, with boring, balding Bryony still going about her monotonous business in the real one.

We met at a bar that overlooked the water and did the sober dance everyone does when they know someone well enough to snog them only when drunk – a peck on the cheek, the odd brush against one another when ordering drinks, the wonderful, almost breathtaking anticipation of what might happen after a few more. We spoke about our families. I bored him with the minutiae of my parents' divorce, and he said, 'God, this isn't boring at all. Mine broke up when I was younger so I know what you're going through.' Lots of people in the world have parents who have divorced, and you don't jump into bed with them all on account of this, but I told myself that this was a sign that he was a kindred spirit, my saviour even. The sun went down, we got more and more pissed, and we started to smooch – oh God, I just used the word smooch! – and then, when the bell rang for last orders, he did it.

He asked me if I wanted to go back to his.

It makes me sick now to think of his hands on me, his tongue in my mouth or roaming around my body. When I think of sex with him it makes me physically shudder, and not in a good way, even though it can't have at the time. In my mind, he's bearing down on another person, he's possessing someone else, because that can't be me, can it, willingly allowing this violent man to fuck me? I look at that version of me, and I want to shout 'WHAT WERE YOU THINKING?!' but the truth is I wasn't thinking at all. I was feeling. And feeling without thinking can be dangerous; it's like being off your tits on drugs.

So as I sit here, writing about those early days of our relationship, I can't help but feel a bit uncomfortable – uncomfortable and embarrassed, because . . . well, I don't really know why. I do not want to revisit my time with him, but revisit it I must, because it probably explains a lot, and at the very least someone might read it and pluck up the courage to walk out on their bloodsucker, on the person feasting on their self-esteem.

'Do you want to come back to mine?' he said, and I must have been feeling brave from the alcohol, because I told him I did. I told him I did but I did not tell him I'd had sex just once before, because I didn't want to spoil it. I didn't want to ruin the mood. I just wanted to get it out of the way. I was buoyed by the events of the last few days. I was on a roll. I could do this! I totally could!

We made our way to the tube station, holding hands as we went, and I started to fret silently about what would happen when he inevitably realised that I was frigid and in possession of hips that didn't move in the right way, and legs that didn't wrap around his body like a serpentine porn star. My train of thought was thankfully interrupted by a male voice thundering 'FUCK!' so loudly that it almost sounded as if it had come from right next to me. It almost sounded as if it had come from Paul. Startled, I turned to him, and realised with a growing sense of horror that it had. Paul had let go of my hand and was standing there staring at the whiteboard that had been placed in front of the ticket gates, and he was effing and blinding so hard that I felt the cold shock of sobriety shoot through me.

The whiteboard proclaimed that the Jubilee line had been suspended. 'FUCKING FUCK FUCK!' shouted Paul at the inanimate object, before finding a London Underground worker to turn his ire on. 'WHY THE FUCK HAS THIS HAPPENED?' he shouted at a man who looked just as taken aback as I felt. Sure, people lose their shit when the tube goes down. It's annoying. It's an inconvenience. But this . . . this was not your normal response to the suspension of the Jubilee line, even in the far reaches of the London Docklands. It was on a completely different level. It was as if someone had left a note on the whiteboard announcing that all his family had been kidnapped and murdered.

'Sir, I think you should cal—' began the man, but he didn't have a chance to finish.

'DO NOT TELL ME TO CALM DOWN,' shouted Paul, whose pre-empting of the man's words told me that he was somewhat used to hearing them. I stepped away, shocked and scared. I couldn't quite believe what was happening, that this charming, handsome man who moments earlier had been regaling me with stories about the idiots he worked with was now exploding in a thankfully not-quite-violent rage. 'HOW. THE. FUCK. DO. YOU. EXPECT. US. TO. GET. HOME?' he hollered into the cavernous hall of Canary Wharf tube station.

The man from London Underground stepped back just as Paul punched the whiteboard. At this I had to interject. 'Paul, stop it!' I said, trying to hold him back as he turned his fists on the innocent piece of plastic and metal. He turned to me and seemed to realise what was happening; he seemed to calm down. 'I'm sorry,' he said, as he started to walk speedily towards the tube exit, me trying frantically to catch up while mumbling apologies in the direction of the worker, who looked at me with pity I didn't deserve, pity I didn't warrant because at that point I was just a date. I wasn't his girlfriend. At that point, I could have walked away. I could have stopped chasing him, cut my losses and gone to catch the bus home. But my losses seemed so huge, and I had become so used to them, that I was even terrified of losing them. They were part of the very fabric of me.

We got a cab back to his in stony silence. I couldn't work out how he had gone from being massively over-keen on me to this. Had he had some kind of epiphany while walking to the tube station, and realised that he was about to sleep with a mousy loser with an eating disorder? Had he seen an alopecia patch and felt nothing but pure revulsion? Was I now making things worse by continuing to tag along like some lamentable limpet? My head swam with all the miserable possibilities of what I had done wrong, without it once occurring to me that I had nothing to do with it. Me, me, me. It was all my fault.

Pathetically, I still hoped something might happen. I hoped that we would walk through the door of his neat little two-bed flat, that he would apologise and tell me he was on medication or something and shouldn't have been drinking, that he would then take me to his bed and make love to me, thus eradicating everything that had happened at the tube station. I still hoped for my happy ending. But of course it didn't happen that way. We got to his, and he said that he wasn't feeling great, and while he was really sorry for what had happened, maybe it would be better if I slept in the spare room. Everything about him asked, 'Why are you here?' but I still hung around like cheap perfume, desperate to cling to him and seep into him through his pores. Meekly I went where I was told without so much as a polite direction to the bathroom, or a 'help yourself to whatever you want'. There was a single bed in the room, with scratchy horrible linen that was probably as old as me, but nothing else. Not a single poster or book or side table.

That night, in the dark, empty room, I did not sleep. I lay there and tried to work out what had gone wrong. I told myself it was the alcohol's fault, it was the tube's fault, it was my fault for making him come all the way to Canary Wharf. If only we'd met closer to his flat . . .

But it didn't matter, because in the morning he walked me to the tube, and he said that while it had been nice getting to know me, he thought that maybe it would be better if we didn't see each other again.

'Yeah, OK,' I said, trying not to cry. And then I went back to my flat and did exactly that.

It's pathetic, isn't it, but I spend the next two weeks wondering what I have done wrong. Those confident, cool girls at the party, they would have called up their friends and howled with laughter at their lucky escape from Patrick bloody Bateman. But me? I can't help but see the good side in Patrick bloody Bateman. I mean, I am an obsessive compulsive bulimic with alopecia who seems to be incapable of helping herself. I am collecting problems like a magnet does metal shavings.

So when Paul calls two weeks later, seemingly out

of the blue, to tell me he has made a terrible mistake, what do you think I do? Do I a) tell him he has, indeed, made a terrible mistake in messing with me, and then hang up the phone and get on with my life?; or b) feel flooded with such relief and gratitude that I immediately agree to see him again without so much as even mentioning the whiteboard incident, or the silent taxi back to his, or the sad, creepy little room he made me sleep in, because hey, who hasn't made mistakes in their time?

I think you can guess what option I decide to take – the one-way ticket to Miseryville. If Paul was looking for a weak-willed woman, clearly he had won the jackpot with me. He had won the fucking rollover lottery. Perhaps this was his wooing tactic – behave appallingly, see if the girl reacts, ignore her for a fortnight, then beg her to come back, somehow, inexplicably, making her feel special in the process.

For the next few months, Paul is a dream. The tube station incident really does seem to be an anomaly. We go out in Soho, get drunk on each other, and I even gather up the (inebriated) courage to tell him I am new to all of this. I, um, have only ever had sex once before and that was years ago. And do you know what he says? He says, 'I'm glad you trust me enough to feel able to tell me this kind of thing, because I wouldn't want to sleep with someone who didn't trust me in that way.' Vomit. And speaking of which, for a while, my bulimia seems to disappear, perhaps because I am so lovestruck I can't actually eat. Still, in my head, this is a sign that Paul is good for me. He is just the tonic I need. He even tells me that my alopecia doesn't bother him one bit.

This is the kind of place I was in, one where I really believed that a bit of exposed scalp might be enough to make someone dislike me.

The sex is perfunctory, but as it is the only sex I really know I tell Chloe that it is absolutely amazing. Paul and I see each other every night, and the more I don't see the whiteboard side of him, the more I forget it ever existed. We spend hours in the pub, watch endless movies at his, and at the weekend I pretend I am enthralled by the record markets he takes me round, where he is on a constant hunt for Bob Dylan bootlegs. He spends hours in bed, playing me Dylan's music, and I swoon at the romance of it all even if deep down I cannot stand a single one of his songs and would rather be listening to nails on a blackboard. But I stomach the Bob Dylan because Paul is so caring, so kind. He buys me Agent Provocateur underwear, and dresses he thinks I will look pretty in. That's what good men do, isn't it? Treat their women like shop mannequins . . .

After four or five months, it becomes clear that things are serious. One night, drunkenly – we are always drunk, like all new couples, right? – Paul suggests I move in. We are spending so much time together that it makes sense in every way. What's the point of having two toothbrushes, or paying two sets of rent? We meet each other's parents. My mother is almost as happy as I am that her first-born has met such a dashing, handsome guy. So I try to ignore the ex-girlfriend Paul always mentions late at night, because hey, why dwell on stuff like that? I move my things in. I pay no attention when he mentions how I do things differently from her – how I brush my teeth, how she used to make him healthy, low-fat dinners, while all we seem to eat is takeaway. I drown it out. I have a job, and a boyfriend I am living with. There's no going back now.

Relationships like this, they creep up on you slowly. They wouldn't happen any other way. Like praying mantises, they dance seductively in front of you to lure you in before biting your head off. They work by stealth, and before you know it you are declaring undying love to a man who seems sometimes to hate you. Except what you're feeling isn't love, not really. It's fear. It's fear of him, fear of yourself, fear of being alone. It feeds on every single one of your myriad insecurities. It feeds on them, and then it uses them as a breeding ground to create even more. Things you didn't even know bothered you start to become an issue. The way you walk. Your habit of breathing heavily when you sleep. The sound of your cry, which has become so normal you almost can't hear it any more.

A few months after I move in, he leaves his mark on me for the first time. I have gone out with friends on a hot Friday night in August, shortly after I have turned twenty-one, and I am in a good mood when I leave the pub to catch the tube home. I am in such a good mood that before venturing underground, I buy a couple of bottles of cheap white wine, imagining us drinking them in the garden while chain-smoking fags and looking forward to the weekend. We have a Sunday lunch with some of his friends, and plans to go clubbing with Chloe on Saturday night. Perhaps we can meet in a bar beforehand, or go round to hers with a bottle of cava or three.

As I walk up the road to our flat – his flat, really – I become dimly aware of a figure sitting on the front steps and realise it is Paul. I up my pace to an inebriated skip, start to sing 'Happy Friday' to the tune of Happy Birthday, and begin to take one of the bottles of Soave (urghh!) out of my handbag to wave in front of him. But as I reach the small path leading to the front door, it immediately becomes clear that Paul is not in any mood to celebrate. He stands up, his hands balled into fists, and as he comes towards me I notice that his once-handsome face is now snarled up like an angry Rottweiler. I instinctively back away from the man I am supposed to love but it is too late. He has taken the bottle of wine from my hands and smashed it onto the road. He has reached into my handbag for the other one and flung that to the ground too. An explosion of glass and the smell of cheap alcohol surrounds us. 'WHERE THE FUCK HAVE YOU BEEN?' he shouts at me, pushing me into the road, and I am ashamed to say that in that moment what I feel is not anger or injustice but embarrassment. I do not want the neighbours to see, do not want a passer-by to get involved.

'NOW YOU COME HOME, NOW YOU DO,' he rages, and all I can do is stutter that I have been with friends, I told him I was going out, he knew, and then he snatches my handbag, empties it on to the pavement, fishes out the keys, grabs me so hard he actually pinches me, and drags me towards the flat, one arm unlocking the door, the other locked around me, and then he pulls me inside, rips off a leather necklace my mother had bought me from Selfridges for my twenty-first birthday, and pushes me on to the bed.

'I DIDN'T HAVE KEYS,' he screams. 'YOU DIDN'T HAVE YOUR PHONE ON SO I HAVE SAT HERE FOR AN HOUR WAITING FOR YOU TO COME HOME. AND WHEN YOU DO YOU ARE ALL HAPPY AS IF NOTHING HAS FUCKING HAPPENED. HOW FUCKING DARE YOU? HOW FUCKING FUCKING DARE YOU?' I try to get up and he grabs me around the top of my arms to keep me in my place.

'I'm sorry,' I mutter. 'I was on the tube . . . I couldn't have known you had forgotten your key—'

'DON'T FUCKING MAKE UP EXCUSES YOU FUCKING BITCH,' and then he pushes me back to the bed, collapses on it next to me and starts to cry.

Somehow, I find myself comforting him.

In the morning I wake up and he has gone. Is it strange that this scares me, and I am fearful he has left me? When I hear the key in the door, I am flooded with relief. He walks into the room holding a small Selfridges bag, sits next to me on the bed and puts his arms around me.

'I'm so sorry,' he says.

'It's OK,' I reassure him.

'I got you this.' He hands me the bag.

'You shouldn't have,' I actually say, even though it is the least he could do.

In the bag is a replica of the necklace my mother bought me for my twenty-first, the one he tore from my neck the night before. I feel a surge of euphoria that he has done this for me, despite the fact that the only reason he has done this for me is because of what he did to me a few hours earlier. We have sex. We go out for brunch. We have more sex. We go clubbing with Chloe.

'I broke my necklace last night drunkenly,' I tell Chloe, 'and the sweetest thing is that before I had even got up, Paul had gone and bought me a new one.' She nods along, although I am not sure she can hear me transforming him from a sinner into a saint over the music. It is 33 degrees in the club, possibly 35, and yet I am wearing a long-sleeved top. I am wearing a long-sleeved top to hide the purple imprints of Paul's fingers on my arms.

Sometimes Paul loses it when we are on a night out, and these are the moments I live in fear of – the ones where he shows his true colours in front of others and explodes the myth I have created of a happy young couple living together in unwedded bliss. When he does it just with me, behind closed doors, it almost doesn't matter because, hey, it's only me. But in front of friends it becomes more problematic. It threatens to ruin the narrative I have created and somehow I feel it reflects badly on me. It's as if I'm the reason he is like this. 'Paul doesn't normally behave this way,' I will say, as we are forced to leave another event because he has put his fist through a pub window, or kicked over a Christmas tree. 'Next time let's meet in the day for lunch.' My friends nod politely. I try to ignore the fact that they would clearly rather chew off their own arms than spend another moment with me and my boyfriend.

There's the time he takes a swing at Chloe's boyfriend because he thinks he's staring at my tits, and there's the evening out with some of my old school friends when he seems to lose the plot simply out of boredom. At home one night, after some people have been round for drinks, he slams my arm in the garden door – I really can't remember why, and nor should it really matter – and then when I scream, he locks me outside in the cold for ten long minutes that feel like days. While I am out there, he calls an ambulance to humiliate me, to teach me and my tears a lesson. 'If it's that bad, then I'd better call the emergency services,' he sneers from the other side of the glass. They arrive and put frozen peas on my arm, and Paul gives me a look that says, 'Told you you were making a fuss.'

It's true. I do appear always to be making a fuss. I am emotional, crazy, drinking too much, because who would want to be sober for all of this? I seem to thrive on the chaos. It's as if I am powered by it. I loathe drama now but aged twenty-one I mistake it for passion, an inevitable symptom of being completely head over heels in love. 'You bring out the worst in me,' he says, and he's right, isn't he? When I met him he was this handsome, charming man who only ever had the decency to try to make me feel special. Now I have turned him into a monster.

All my energy is spent on pleasing him, turning him into the man he was when we first met. If he tells me I should go for a run in the pouring rain, I will go for a run in the pouring rain. If he tells me I need to do another fifty lengths of the pool, I will do another fifty lengths of the pool. If he tells me not to put my hair into a half-ponytail because it makes me look like Mel

Gibson in *Braveheart*, then I won't put my hair into a half-ponytail, because clearly I look like Mel Gibson in *Braveheart*. (This is what I am dealing with – a man who belittles me with humour.)

I am so completely devoted to not upsetting him that anxiety becomes my default setting. I am secretly back to throwing up again, terrified he will hear me, but if he does he never mentions it. I become consumed with the worry that I too am turning into some sort of monster. I worry that someone is trapped in the basement, and check it fifteen times a day. I am, quite literally, in a bad place.

He tells me I have to go on the pill, and while I am at the doctor's surgery I take the opportunity to ask if it might be possible to go back on antidepressants for a bit, the ones I stopped taking when we got together because I was high on Paul. Coolly, calmly, I explain to the doctor my background of mental-health issues and my worry that things are creeping up on me again, and he writes me a prescription for some Citalopram without even looking at me.

Is it the pill or the Citalopram that makes me hysterical, or is it Paul? I suspect now it was the latter but at the time I blame my erratic, tearful behaviour on a bad combination of medication. Paul thinks it is a good idea me being on antidepressants, and I am pretty sure that is because it is some sort of vindication for him, proof that I am the cause of all the madness in our relationship. My mental-health issues are the perfect cover for his mental-health issues, if you will. With me by his side, everything makes sense to people. I am basically his way of saying, 'Look at my mad girlfriend with her antidepressants and her OCD and her alopecia! It's no wonder I lose it from time to time, frankly!'

Our relationship soon takes on a familiar pattern. We go out, I do something wrong, he tells me he is leaving me, we make up, repeat to fade. It is never, ever me who threatens to go. I convince myself we are a modern-day Richard Burton and Elizabeth Taylor, because that is how deluded I now am. No, deluded isn't the right word, because this type of relationship is all that I know. I turn twenty-two. I turn twenty-three. Years go by without me even realising that I am being worn down. I think it is perfectly normal for your boyfriend to call you stupid, or fat, or pathetic. Hey, I tell myself, these are just things said in the heat of the moment. I seem actually to enjoy it that afterwards, when the dust has settled and his red mist has evaporated, he strokes my hair and tells me how beautiful I could be if I just made a bit more of an effort. Wow, I think, check out how nice he's being to me.

This, I now recognise, is just the chemical flood experienced by an obsessive compulsive brain when it gets the reassurance it is always craving.

I am on edge 24/7, waiting to see what Paul I will

get – caring, funny Paul, or cross, worked-up Paul – but I have no idea how highly strung I am. Without even being aware of it, I become very good at acting, at putting on a smile and a cheery face. Paul is good at it, too. When we are with our families, we are the golden couple who can do no wrong. My parents, now divorced and living separately, applaud me for managing to have such a wonderful, grounded relationship.

It ends quite by accident, this strange period of my life. We go out to the pub with his old university friends and there, for the first time, is the hallowed ex he mentions so often. The one who cooked for him, and apparently gave him blow jobs morning noon and night. The one who had legs like a supermodel's, legs that ran marathons and did triathlons and were adorned with high heels while he fucked her over the kitchen table.

Her name is Sophie. For years I have rolled that name around my head – isn't it so charming? – while imagining the goddess who came before me. Paul and Sophie. Paul and Sophie. Paul and Sophie. Urgghh, they even sounded perfect together. I hated Sophie with every fibre of my body but now she sits in front of me and the scales drop. She looks friendly, sweet. Buoyed by beer, I decide to speak to her, to break the ice, and show her there are no hard feelings. I think that Paul will be impressed by this. I think he will see it as a sign of how mature I am, what a catch I am.

She is warm and welcoming when I introduce myself. We discuss the work we do, the dresses we are wearing, and then, raging up like a monster behind Sophie, I see Paul with that by-now familiar look on his face. He elbows me in the side and stands between us, and he says to me, very calmly, 'What the hell do you think you're doing?'

This is when I feel really scared. He isn't shouting. He isn't effing and blinding and throwing things around. All there is now is pure hatred in his eyes.

'I'm sorry, Sophie,' he says, manoeuvring to take me away. 'I hope she wasn't bothering you.'

And Sophie, with whom I am still friends on Facebook all these years later, does her own manoeuvre to keep me exactly where I am.

'Actually, Paul,' she says, a look as sweet as pie on her face, 'Bryony isn't bothering me at all. But you are. Please leave us alone.'

Well, that does it.

Paul erupts, throwing his pint of beer to the floor, not for the first time – but thankfully, for the last time – spraying me with shards of glass and stinking booze. The room goes quiet. A male friend goes to pull him away but is pushed off. Another, bigger, stronger guy weighs in and tells Paul that he needs to leave. I am mortified. Horrified. I feel my world ending, the curtains being pulled shut on this particular act of my life. 'IF YOU THINK YOU'RE COMING BACK TO

Mad Girl

THE FLAT, YOU CAN GET FUCKED,' he screams at me as he is pulled out of the pub. 'WE'RE FINISHED. I NEVER WANT TO FUCKING SEE YOU AGAIN. YOU'VE HUMILIATED ME.'

'He's humiliated himself,' Sophie whispers in my ear.

And then I begin to cry. There, in the middle of the bar, with my ex-boyfriend's ex-girlfriend and a group of people I barely know, I start to bawl my eyes out.

'You're coming with me,' says Sophie, who has gathered my bag and my coat and is guiding me to the door. Outside she hails a cab and bundles us inside it, giving the driver her address and handing me tissues so that I can wipe away my tears and snot and mascara. God, I am so tired of that toxic combination of tears and snot and mascara. She keeps her arm around me the whole way to her flat, pays for the journey, and takes me inside where she makes camomile tea and sits me on her sofa.

'I know what he's like,' she says. 'I've been there. The temper, the tantrums, the eruptions. He'll make you think it's your fault. If it wasn't for you, he'd be a paragon of fucking virtue. But the only person who makes him the way he is is himself. Nobody else is to blame. For two years I put up with his shit and I feel like a fucking fool for it. Don't let him make you think that this is somehow a new thing and he was never this way before.'

In my bag, my phone is bleeping. It is Paul, telling me not to listen to Sophie and her lies. 'Switch it off,' says Sophie, and I do listen to her, this kind woman who has gone out of her way to make me feel better, who has made me tea and given me tissues and hugged me. She puts me in her spare room, this one bright and homely and festooned in fairy lights. 'Stay here tonight. You can't go back to his.'

And I don't. I never stay another night at Paul's. I go and get my stuff when he is at work, and I tell my mother what he was really like, and although I am broken and emotionally battered, for the first time in a long time, I feel safe.

Sophie, I should tell you, is now happily married with a family. I have no idea what has happened to Paul, and nor do I want to know. A few months after I finally break up with him, I meet a bloke called Sam. Sam is kind and sweet and has a sense of humour that doesn't rely on being horrible to me. I never once see him get cross, never once feel on edge while on a night out with him, and never once wonder what version of him I am going to get.

Soon after we meet, he brings me breakfast in bed. I am completely and utterly dumbstruck by this gesture. 'Why did you do that?' I ask him, after I have downed the orange juice and stuffed myself with eggs and bacon. He looks confused. 'Why wouldn't I do that?

That's what you do when you like someone – nice things.'

It is an important lesson I am glad to learn. We break up eventually, when he moves to Edinburgh, and I weep for his kindness. I feel a million times more heartbroken than I ever did with Paul – because with Paul I only ever wept because I had lost myself, whereas with Sam I weep because I have lost him.

And as I am going through that heartbreak, I go to a party thrown by a mutual friend of mine and Paul's. I am dimly aware that he might be there but I reason that I am not going to let this stop me seeing my mates. Sure enough, I spot him across the room. I ignore him, but he finds me, seeks me out like an angry missile.

'I hear you got dumped by that bloke,' he shouts over the music. 'Was it because you're so fat?'

Reader, at this point I am a size ten.

I take a deep breath and tell him to go away. Our mutual friend, who is standing nearby, sees this conversation and comes over to try to move Paul away. Paul pushes him to the floor. A security guard comes over and grabs my hideous, unhinged ex, but before he is removed from the party, he has one more parting shot for me.

'Nobody will ever love you the way I did,' he shouts.

And all I can think is thank heavens for that. Thank the fucking heavens.

7

I think I might be having too good a time

Now I know what you're thinking at this point. You're thinking, where are the laughs? Where are the jokes, the fun stories, the witty anecdotes? Where's the light relief? We've had OCD, alopecia, bulimia, divorce and domestic abuse . . . please, Bryony, give us a break! Give us something to cling to, some hope that everything is going to turn out all right in the end.

Well, OK then.

It hasn't all been vomit, bruises and low self-esteem. Writing this, I realise how miserable I sound, what a dreary human being I must come across as. I'm amazed you've actually managed to make it this far, a whole seven chapters in, without losing the will to read. Hello, hello, hello! Are you still there? Can you hear me?

Anyone?

Anyone?

Anyone at all?

At school there is always that one person who has something permanently wrong with them, isn't there? She can't take part in PE because of some mystery ailment you suspect is completely made up. If you've got a headache, she's got a suspected brain tumour, et cetera et cetera. But now I wonder if that person is me. I wonder if you're calling me a drama queen as you hold me in your hands. I bet you're rolling your eyes when you think I'm not looking. You're probably sighing loudly every time I come out with another chapter about the-time-I-thought-I-had-killed-some-one-blah-blah-blah-yada-yada-yada and so on and so on. Poor me, poor me, pour me another drink. Why is it that most people who suffer from mental illness can't just make do with the one? Why can't we be happy with a generalised anxiety disorder, or a problem with food, or a desire to self-harm? There's always more, isn't there? One leads to another, each mental illness a gateway to bigger, nastier ones that will *really* fuck us up this time.

Sigh.

So before I get on to writing about my reliance on Class A drugs, I'd like first to tell you about how great my life is, in tandem with all of this. It's very important for me to stress this because a) I am still needy and insecure and want you to like me, and b) as I said earlier, mental illness does not always fit the binary, black-and-white terms given to it in the media, books and films. This is also why it is such a bastard. It is good at hiding, evading capture, putting on a show. It is the world's greatest actor. Its ability to convince people it is something it is not is completely unparalleled. Laurence Olivier could have taken lessons from it. Leonardo di Caprio trails in its wake.

So people who suffer from it are not always rocking back and forth in a padded cell. I'm definitely not. I have graduated from teen section to main paper and am now a sort of grown-up feature writer on the *Daily Telegraph*, living in a dank basement flat with my sister and a family of silverfish who won't budge from the bathroom, but let us try to overlook that particular detail for a moment. After a while, we certainly did. I have my dream job, and feel like the luckiest girl in the world. By day I work with some of the most talented people on Fleet Street, and by night I drink with them. It's as if I have landed on my feet in shiny new Christian Louboutin heels, not that I could ever actually afford them.

The OCD is there – it always is, my phrases playing like background music in a department store – and there are days when I wonder if I can get out of bed. But I get good at hiding the horrors in my head. As you will soon see, I become the perennial party girl with a smile almost permanently slapped on her face. On an almost daily basis, I am wrapped in the candyfloss-soft world that is the fluffy side of the *Telegraph*. This is the kind of content that tedious online commenters would today leave a post underneath saying, 'Are you paid to write this drivel?' (Yes, yes I am. Are you paid to write your comments? No? I win.) 'Why am I reading this when there is a war in Syria?' is another one. (I don't know is the answer. There are plenty of articles about Syria on the *Telegraph* website, so I'm not quite sure why you've clicked on an interview with Kirstie Allsopp hoping to find in-depth analysis of the Assad regime and ISIS.) But thankfully, back at the beginning of my career, digital media was embryonic. I say thankfully because at the brittle age of twenty-four or twenty-five, I am not entirely sure I would have been able to deal with all the online abuse that washes off me like water off a duck's back today. Still, I am a passionate supporter of the need for fluff in papers, because these pieces provide much-needed light after the endless darkness of the news pages, and because it's really OK to be interested in celebrities and fashion and films and music. This doesn't make you a less important person than the one who only ever wants to read about politics and war. Also, having visited the depths of mental illness, I have always had a healthy appreciation for life in the shallow side of the pool, for the stuff that makes you smile, or distracts you from grim realities.

So you can imagine my joy when I am asked to spend a week living like Victoria Beckham, according to a book in which she dispenses her fashion and beauty tips. I get a spray tan, have my hair done every morning, have to wear Louboutins each day (sadly, they must be sent back) and attend the British Fashion Awards dressed in an Hervé Leger frock.

This, people, is my job.

I am dispatched to Iceland to interview Björk, who, after our chat, takes me on an impromptu tour of Reykjavik. She is wearing pom poms on her feet. I am sent to Ladies Day at Ascot wearing something no less silly on my head – a hat made up of a tea set. I go to Harrogate to train with the Green Berets at five in the morning in the cold and the rain, where I am made to crawl through the mud and feel very, very weak. I attempt to learn to dance with Anton du Beke from *Strictly Come Dancing*, although what really happens is I spend a morning stepping on his feet. Another time, I am allowed to raid the costume department of the show to see what it feels like to wear spandex and sequins. This isn't going to win me the Pulitzer Prize any time soon, but it sure is fun.

I am dispatched to walk part of the Great Wall of China with Sir Cliff Richard, Olivia Newton-John and Joan Rivers, who are doing it for charity. Joan arrives and immediately announces that she thought she was going to the Great Mall of China. Later, I find myself helping her into a loo that is actually a latrine, and holding the door for her. She picks me a bunch of flowers as a thank-you gesture afterwards, and then Sir Cliff starts singing 'Summer Holiday' to distract from the lorry load of dead dogs that has just driven past us.

I am sent around the world in eight days with Richard Branson. My boss decides that before I go, I must be photographed dressed up as a Virgin trolley-dolly for the pictures to accompany the piece. These photos still exist somewhere on the internet, but I beg you please do not Google 'Bryony Gordon Virgin'. We travel to Hong Kong, Sydney, Los Angeles, flying everywhere in upper class, where there is a bar and they give you pyjamas and actual, proper cutlery, because clearly the very, very rich can be trusted not to try to rush the cockpit to boff the pilots over the head with spoons. It is so amazing that I am momentarily cured of my fear of flying, which just goes to show you how irrational it is. The chances of the plane going down are the same whatever class you happen to be travelling in, but I suppose if it happens up front, you can at the very least drink champagne as you plummet to your death.

Here, I feel duty bound to mention all the ridiculous rituals that I have to complete when getting on a plane. I can only pack and wear clothes that have travelled in the air with me before, in a bag that has travelled in the air with me before, because clearly this makes them immune from air disasters. This is also why, to this very day, I have a suitcase so old it is almost falling apart and a handbag that was last in fashion in 2002.

Once at the airport I have to chant 'the plane will land safely' over and over again, think of two places beginning with L that aren't Lockerbie (Lille, Los Angeles), imagine two singers beginning with B who aren't Buddy Holly (Bryan Adams, Brian Harvey – how apt that the unhinged one from East 17 should be part of my pre-flight ritual) and focus on two films I have seen in which people have travelled safely on an aeroplane. Currently, these are *The Holiday* and *Bridget Jones: The Edge of Reason*.

In Sydney, Branson throws a party and abseils into it down a very high building (I don't need to tell you that I am scared of heights, do I?). The next day we journalists go by seaplane to a restaurant in a cove where we drink wine over lunch. We drink champagne all the way from Sydney to Los Angeles, where we land before we actually took off, and use the hours we have gained to drink more champagne at another lavish party, before collapsing into our beds at a hotel in Beverly Hills that has thoughtfully monogrammed my initials on all the pillowcases.

After that, every time I fly Virgin I find myself upgraded, and one time, on a trip back from New York, I am actually seated next to Hugh Jackman, who turns to me and says – and I am absolutely NOT making this up – 'Has anyone ever told you that you look a bit like Kate Winslet?' to which I reply, 'Has anyone ever told you that you look a bit like Hugh Jackman?' Oh, how we laugh! Later in the flight there is turbulence so bad that even the cabin crew are ordered to put their seat belts on, and all I can think is, 'I am going to die without being able to tell anyone I was sitting next to Hugh Jackman. I am going to die without being able to tell anyone I was sitting next to Hugh Jackman. Oh well. At least I am going to die sitting next to Hugh Jackman, and hopefully it will show up in the passenger manifest. Then my mother can take some comfort that I went just as I had always wanted to – next to a major celebrity while drinking champagne.' That didn't occur, obviously, but I did manage to get a picture of us together before we landed as proof that this totally fantastical thing did actually happen.

I'm beginning to sound like a name-dropper here, and perhaps a tad arrogant, but I once got sent to Los Angeles to interview Justin Timberlake for twenty minutes. Over 5,000 miles they flew me for a meeting that lasted less time than it takes to have a nice bath. What pearls of wisdom did I glean from him in that time? That he was very spiritual, which he told me as he lit a candle.

'I'm really spontaneous,' he announced, a moment

later. 'Like, let's go and finish this interview in that tree.'

'OK!' I beamed, standing up and making my way to the garden of the villa. Justin Timberlake looked at me with something approaching pity in his eyes. (Now there's a sentence I never thought I would ever write.)

'Um, I was only, like, joking,' he said.

I get to spend a little longer in LA on another occasion when work send me to cover the build-up to the Oscars, and the glittering party that Sir Elton John throws after the ceremony. For this I am fitted for a dress by designer Suzanne Neville, a creation that costs more than I take home in six months. I stay at the Mondrian on Sunset Boulevard and go to the 'gift suites' set up all over Beverly Hills, where very rich actors and actresses are given expensive things they can well afford for free. I get my hair done on Rodeo Drive, and attend a party thrown by Soho House in the Hollywood Hills. There is free-flowing champagne and canapes that nobody but me seems to eat.

I sneak outside to a balcony to have a cigarette where, almost impossibly, I am confronted by Robbie Williams, who is also smoking a fag.

'Hi, I'm Robbie,' he says, reaching to shake my hand.

My hand, of all the hands in the world!

'I know,' I squeak.

'What's your name?' he actually asks me.

Me, of all people!

'I can't remember,' I think, but eventually I manage to pluck it from the recesses of my completely shocked mind. Then he starts talking to me about Chelsea's chances of winning the premiership, which is not how I had imagined this going, not, of course, that I had ever imagined this going at all. I try, frantically, to compose some sort of football chat, to prove that I am just the girl he wants to marry – a cool, calm one who can name at least two members of the Chelsea squad. Frank Lampard, and, um . . . It doesn't matter. Before I have a chance, a tall blonde with pneumatic boobs rushes into his arms and I am seemingly forgotten about, left smoking awkwardly before exiting the balcony to find more booze.

Story of my life.

Later, at the Elton John party, I see Paris Hilton dressed up as some sort of peacock. Everyone is – strutting and preening like they belong in the zoo. I am surrounded by the surgically enhanced, people whose superpowers involve never being able to smile, and for once I feel pleased to have my own body, and not to live in a place where perky plasticness is expected of you.

I return to my hotel and gladly throw off the corseted dress that has left indents in my skin. Relieved to be going back to my sister and the silverfish the next day, I get into bed, only to realise that my beloved blankie, the thing that has come everywhere with me since I was a small child, has disappeared. Vanished. 'Blankie,' I wail, to nobody in particular, noting that I am a twenty-five-year-old woman who still sucks her thumb and has a security blanket, and thus it is not really a surprise that I cannot get a boyfriend. I call down to reception and explain to them that something is missing from my room.

'Would you like us to call security, Mam?' asks the woman on the other end of the phone.

'No, no,' I say, a blush rising up my neck. 'I don't think anyone would have wanted to steal this. It's just a manky old cardigan that I keep as my blankie.'

'Oh,' says the woman. 'I understand. I had a toy elephant and I was devastated when I lost it.'

I feel relief to have found a kindred spirit.

'I was five,' she adds.

I reason that it must have been taken accidentally by housekeeping, so I ring and ask if they have discovered my manky old cardigan among the towels and sheets.

'You're what?' they ask.

'A manky old cardigan,' I repeat.

'What's manky?'

'My cardigan is.'

'Is it a brand, Mam?'

And round and round we go.

They have not got my manky old cardigan. Blankie is clearly the only companion I will ever have, and even he has legged it at the earliest possible opportunity. I call my mother, because it is the morning in the UK and she will understand what I am going through. 'I've lost him!' I actually cry down the phone, and I cannot work out what is more disturbing – the fact I am in my mid-twenties and sobbing about a blankie, or the fact I have just given it a gender.

'You've just spent a night at Elton John's Oscar party and you have called me to tell me you've lost a thread-bare cardigan I bought from Benetton over two decades ago?'

'There's no way I can leave LA without him!'

But leave LA I must, without Blankie, whom I imagine living it up around the pool with his new girlfriend Hotel Towelie. I sit crammed into my economy seat at the back of the plane next to the toilets, next to a Russian woman who won't stop crying because, as I later discover, her documentary about orphaned children in Moscow failed to win the Oscar it was nominated for. That puts things into perspective a bit.

An hour into the flight, as I try to comfort the sobbing Russian woman, the captain comes over the Tannoy to tell us that the flight is being diverted due to an emergency. 'First I no win, now we die!' wails my travelling companion, not entirely helpfully. Soon we learn that it is because someone has fallen ill, and as we land in Salt Lake City, where we get to spend several hours without ever leaving the plane, I tell myself that this is all my fault and it wouldn't have happened if Blankie had been with me still. Thus I reinforce my completely mental belief that the clothes I wear and the items I pack are somehow capable of magically safe-proofing an entire 300-tonne Boeing 747 and all the people within it.

We take off, land safely, and I eventually get over the loss of Blankie, although I think of him often, on his sun lounger by the pool. And despite being very clearly unhinged, my career seems to thrive. I am given a column, and nominated for young journalist of the year at the Press Awards. I go on press trips to the Maldives, Dubai and Thailand, staying in places that cost more for one night than my dank basement flat does for a month. And I am happy, I think. Certainly I look back at this time and think how exciting it was, and how unbelievably fortunate I was to have all these experiences. Although earlier I wrote that you create your own luck, I do have a feeling that in my twenties some fairy godmother was watching over me, making sure I came to no harm. Because even as I was lucky, I was also very stupid.

When I look back on the first decade of my adult life, it is not defined by these career highs, as wonderful and fun as they were. Those years are defined by illegal highs. They are defined by drugs, the stunningly stupid practice of self-medication, of numbing the pain with pharmaceuticals prescribed to you not by a doctor, but by yourself, and sold to you by a complete stranger. Cocaine was my thing. Not ecstasy, which I tried once or twice but which just made me feel a bit spaced out – something I have never needed help with. And not marijuana, which has only ever had the effect of making me feel down, down, down – another reaction I have never needed to pay money to experience. No. Cocaine was the thing, the one that made me feel up, up, up. Blow. Bugle. Gak. Toot. Powder. Whatever you want to call it, and I've called it everything, coke was my poison. That and alcohol. Combined, they made me feel invincible, at least until the next day, when they combined to make me feel like I was going to die. (Science fact: combining cocaine with alcohol can actually make you die, the two chemicals creating a third chemical, cocaethylene, which can build up in your liver and cause heart attacks. Also, you don't need to be an expert to know that taking cocaine and alcohol and antidepressants is just really fucking stupid, the problem being that people in a really bad place often do behave really fucking stupidly.)

At almost every stage of my twenties, cocaine was there, a comfort and a crutch and also a curse. It was the soundtrack to my decade, a low hum forever in my ear, like tinnitus, or a Dido album. Of course, cocaine is the last thing in the world an obsessive compulsive with self-esteem issues should take, but I have found that often in life the last thing you should take is the thing that you most want. Chocolate. Crisps. The dangerous Class A drug cocaine. They're not that different really, aside from when it comes to their availability in all good supermarkets near you. This is because the qualities that make them so forbidden are precisely the ones that you want more than anything in the world.

After the break-up with Paul I am reinvigorated. There is a whole world out there he never let me see because he was too busy shouting at me in our flat, and I am desperate to see it. I come out of my shell. I am a caterpillar suddenly transformed into a butterfly. Chloe, who has also broken up with her boyfriend, is in a similar mood. Together we hit the town, but instead of painting it red, we paint it a bright, sparkling white. And so it is that I embark on the most meaningful relationship of my twenties, the one I have with booze and narcotics.

The first time I take cocaine is at Chloe's flat one weekend, when she invites me for 'Sunday lunch'. I am twenty-five. Who suddenly discovers drugs at twenty-five? It's so typical of me to cotton on to something about ten years after everyone else. But back to this lunch. Little do I know, as I make my way to Chloe's trendy east London apartment, that it actually involves me, her and our gay friend James chewing nothing more than the inside of our mouths as we motor through industrial quantities of vodka and drugs. In my pathetically deluded mind I am expecting some sort of grown-up lunch party where we discuss politics and the Middle East while drinking red wine, although I have no idea where I get that impression from, given that Chloe has always come across as a disco queen who likes a good time.

I am, at first, taken aback by the scene that confronts me when I arrive, clutching a bag of Kettle chips and a bunch of wilted flowers from the nearby Tesco Metro, which I mistakenly believe to be the kind of thing grown-ups bring to grown-up lunch parties. It isn't what I had in mind, and it isn't what I expected, to see James at the coffee table hunched over a twelve-inch vinyl copy of an album by Chic, several perfectly chopped lines of white powder beneath him and a pink straw in his right hand. But I am damned if I'm going to show myself up to be a complete square, damned if I'm going to sit quietly in a corner wondering when the food is going to be served as my stomach rumbles. I'm just going to have to get on with it. I'm just going to have to try to fit in. And I want to fit in so badly. After the endless anxiety with Paul, I just want to feel good again.

I wander into the immaculate open-plan living room like this is the most normal thing in the world, people taking drugs while the rest of the country prepares to settle down and watch the *Antiques Roadshow*. 'You need a line, baby,' says James, once he has hoovered up most of the powder on the album with the impressive suction of a Miele Cat and Dog vacuum. I smile meekly.

My stomach tightens from hunger and nerves. What if it gives me a heart attack? Worse, what if I do it wrong and Chloe and James laugh at me and decide they no longer want to be my friend? Literally, I would rather die of a heart attack than have this happen. I am that insecure. I am that insecure that I will do drugs I quite patently shouldn't in an attempt to fit in.

I sit down on the sofa next to James. He pushes the album across the coffee table to me, and hands me the pink straw. I hope he won't see when I wipe it on the underside of a cushion, because as much as I like James, I do not fancy ingesting his snot. Who knows what diseases are contained within it? I kneel over the album, take a deep breath, and then I place the straw over one of the lines of white powder and I snort. The sensation is so immediately, madly chemical and unexpected that my eyes start to water and I start to splutter, accidentally blowing the remaining cocaine across the album. I am dimly aware that somewhere in the room James and Chloe are laughing, but I do not care, because right now, I feel fucking great.

And that is that. It was always going to be. What do you get the balding, obsessive compulsive bulimic who has everything? A drug habit, doh! On cocaine I am not me. I am a much better version of me. I am me but sexier, spunkier, sassier. I am me without the OCD, me without the fear. All the stuff that mattered a moment before I snorted that line simply ceases to exist. Sniffffffff. Ping! On cocaine I can do things that minutes before I would never have dreamt of doing. I have the guts to crack jokes, flirt, tell really fucking funny stories. Taking cocaine is like putting on a fabulous designer dress. It's like wearing a towering pair of high heels that you can walk in without falling. Of course, there's a fall to come, of course you will feel terrible in the morning, but I am never thinking about the morning, never thinking about tomorrow. I can only think about now, about how to get through it without actually having to think.

On cocaine I don't have to confront any of my problems. I don't have to tell anyone about my OCD, because I can't actually feel it. I don't have to risk the responses I've heard people with mental-health issues usually get when they dare to share them. Things like:

'Can't you just have some ice cream and cheer up?'
And
'Well, at least you're not dying of cancer or anything.'
And
'Just look at everything you've got and how fortunate you are. Just remember how lucky you are to have a roof over your head and not to live in, like, Syria or Ethiopia.'

And

'I had depression too until I found Jesus. Have you ever thought of finding Jesus?'

On cocaine you can forget about the big problems and worry about the small stuff. You can bury all your massive issues – bulimia, alopecia, the fact you have to pray to the universe every day to keep your family alive – under a thousand tiny ones. What did I say to so-and-so last night? Do you think that bloke I met is going to call me? How did I get home? You can fill your brain with trifling, useless worries in an effort to distract yourself from the important ones. Cocaine is what I use to quieten my OCD – later, I learn that it is not uncommon for these two to go side by side – and it is what I use so I can pretend to everyone that I am happy. They don't need to know that the euphoria is entirely the result of illegal chemicals.

On cocaine the world seems more interesting. I seem more interested. I believe that people are boring when I'm not on it, without seeing the irony that I am the boring one, the one who is increasingly dependent on chemicals to have a good time. On cocaine I do crazy things, and on cocaine I can tell people about these crazy things without feeling any inhibitions whatsoever. I can make them laugh and making people laugh makes me feel good. I am the life of the party without any soul, a performing monkey invited to entertain the crowds with embarrassing tales nobody else would ever dare retell. I am so insecure that I will gladly take these tales about disastrous dates and alcohol blackouts and try to turn them into jokes that make everyone feel better except me. I want to make people happy. I want to make people like me.

Mothers always tell their daughters that nobody likes a girl with a reputation, but I seem to find that the opposite is true. My reputation is the only thing keeping me going. It's the only thing getting me invited to all the best parties. I am incapable of finding my off button because I don't actually seem to be in possession of one. I am always the last girl standing, quite often the last man standing, and I like this reputation, the fact that people like Chloe and James actively want to hang out with me, to hear what crazy thing I have done now. It is addictive, moreish, the only thing I have ever really wanted. And so it is that the idea anyone might want to hang out with non-coke Bryony – the idea that I might want to hang out with non-coke Bryony – quickly disappears.

But it's not like I am taking it every day. Maybe two or three times a week, which is more than most people, but, I tell myself, less than an addict, who would surely be taking it morning, noon and night, right? But that's not me. In the morning I hate cocaine as much as I loved it the night before. I always feel so terrible that I vow not to take it ever again, or at least until the next night out. I never snort it in the office, never have a line to get myself going. So it's easy for me to ignore the telltale signs that my drug-taking has slipped from something recreational to something more habitual. The permanently rolled-up receipt in my wallet, the debit card with coke caked into its embossed numbers. The endless fucking disco cold, the forever streaming nose and scabby nostrils, which I explain away as hayfever in the spring and summer, and being run down at any other time of the year. The lost hours, the forgotten cab journeys home. The unexplained bruises I wake up with, proof that my skin remembers things my brain does not. The fact I have stopped relying on Chloe and James for my drugs, and got a dealer of my own, who calls me darling and drives a family estate car with a child's seat in the back, which I never ask about but assume to be a foil. A dealer I wouldn't recognise in an ID parade, because I am always so out of it and always so desperate to get in and out and back to the party without actually looking at him, without showing him that he is one of the people I call most in my phonebook, without being caught by the police. And all the while the jumpiness, the edginess, the feeling that you are increasingly chasing a high that just does not want to be caught.

My body may be holding up but eventually, when I am twenty-six, my mind collapses under the weight of anxiety. I don't put the way I feel down to all the cocaine I am taking. It doesn't even occur to me. More likely, because I can't believe I would actually be that stupid, I don't allow it to occur to me that cocaine may be the cause of the way I am feeling. I am too dependent on the drug to prop me up and create the myth of fabulous Bryony to let go of it yet. But I am chanting survival prayers as much as I ever have. I am becoming increasingly convinced that while on my benders, I have been so out of it that I have forgotten I've had sex with strangers who have infected me with HIV. Or maybe I killed someone. One morning, I wake up with blood all over my sheets. I have, somehow, sheared off a wart on my knee, and my bed looks like a crime scene. I become tormented that this is what has actually happened. I check the bins for body parts. I rack my brain for evidence of a crime that has not taken place until I am so far gone in this racking of my brain that I start to create what are known as 'false memories' – a common thing in sufferers from OCD, who have spent so much time ruminating, painting horror stories in their heads, that they actually start to believe them. My OCD tells me they are real. I spend my days at work with a fake smile on my face, counting away the hours until I can numb the voices in my head with booze and drugs. I want to die. In desperation, I decide I should try some of that cognitive behaviour therapy that I failed to get a grip on so long ago it feels like another life. I Google CBT, unaware that this is also what the basic motorbike test is known as, and call the nearest place that seems to offer it, somewhere in Vauxhall.

Me (sobbing gently): I wondered if you had any appointments this week for CBT.

Gruff man (sounding only slightly alarmed): Erm, well, we run courses every day except Sunday.

Me (sobbing in relief): Could I come to one tomorrow?

Gruff man: Well, we usually book up quite far in advance [the sound of hysterical crying from me on the other end of the line]. But I'm sure we can see if we can fit you in. Just one moment.

Hold music starts to play. It is the White Snake classic 'Here I Go Again'. I am slightly confused but in need of help so willing to gloss over this most unusual choice of music for a therapy centre. Perhaps they think it will cheer people up?

Gruff man: So I've looked and we don't do this very often but I can hear you are keen to get started so I think we can fit you in on tomorrow's course. Can you remember to bring your provisional licence?

Me: My what?

Gruff man: Your provisional licence. You can't learn to ride a motorbike without one.

Me: Oh. [Hangs up quickly.]

In the end, I find a course run by someone who claims to be able to banish OCD in a weekend. It costs more money than I really have, but I would do anything to be rid of this monster in my head. On the phone, she explains to me that it involves an extreme form of 'exposure' therapy that she has devised, the idea being that if you expose yourself to the things that you fear most, you will eventually start to give them less credence. She sounds mad as a box of frogs, but I reason that this is better than the po-faced therapist I met before, the one who spoke quietly without looking at me, thus serving to make me feel even more mental than I already did.

I take a few days' 'holiday' from work and arrive for the course feeling sick to my stomach. It is held in a basement in a smart part of central London, and I am doing it with an eighteen-year-old boy who has not been able to leave his house for two months, plus a mother in her early thirties who is afraid she has molested her own children. Their presence calms me, but the absence of the woman actually running the course feels slightly strange. She eventually turns up fifteen minutes after the start time, with exquisitely maintained hair, an immaculate face, and wearing the kind of clothes that you see only on shop mannequins in Knightsbridge. She does not apologise for being late. In fact, as the course progresses, it happens again and again and again, until I come to see it as a sort of test by her, to see if we have become brave and strong enough to take her to task on it.

We never do.

On the first day she makes me read out newspaper reports containing the words 'rape' and 'murder'. She tells me to stand up and tell my fellow OCD sufferers that I want my family to die. 'They're just words,' she says, but I cannot utter them without first breaking down in tears.

On day two she takes us to the Natural History Museum, where we have to spend an hour in a room full of dinosaurs and children. The children terrify us most, because what if we accidentally on purpose drag one behind a Stegosaurus and do something awful to it (the child, not the Stegosaurus)? Reader, nothing happens. On day three she makes me tie a banana to a piece of string and walk it down Oxford Street as if it were my pet dog. I have never had a fear of walking bananas down Oxford Street like pet dogs, I argue with my therapist, who, I am now suspecting, might need therapy too. 'I know you don't,' she says, 'but you have a fear of anyone thinking badly of you, and I want you to realise that it doesn't matter what people think of you.' So I walk the banana down Oxford Street. I take it to Waterstones, I take it to Topshop, and by the time I have gone for a snack with it at Pret A Manger, I am beginning to feel quite liberated.

She takes us to Chanel and makes us spend hours trying on clothes with shop assistants even more highly strung than we are, only to tell them, when we go to the counter, that we don't have our wallets on us and would they mind giving us credit until we can come back. I am asked to leave by security. We go on crowded tube carriages where she insists we stand up and shout 'I'M COMPLETELY MENTAL' before sitting back down and carrying on as normal. She makes us lie down on the pavements of busy shopping streets so people have to step around us. It is a bit like starring in an extended episode of a hidden camera show, with the joke being on our therapist. Her methods may well work for some, but they did nothing for me.

At the end of the week we discuss the fact that it is perfectly possible that we are paedophiles, in so much as it is perfectly possible for any human being to be a paedophile, just as it is perfectly possible for any human being to be a serial killer or a master criminal or a petty thief.

'But I don't want to be a paedophile,' I say, not unreasonably.

'Do you think that all paedophiles want to be paedophiles? Some of them are racked with guilt.'

This does not make me feel any better. In fact, I feel more vulnerable, and certainly a lot poorer, by the end of the course, and not in a good way, not in an 'I have faced up to my demons' kind of way. In a deflated, hopeless kind of way. The course ends. I arrange to meet some friends that night for a drink, which turns into a cocaine bender. In my desperation, I have spent a week paying good money to be humiliated, and nothing has changed.

Typical.

Let me tell you about all the ways in which cocaine is disgusting, just in case I am mistakenly making it sound like fun. Cocaine is disgusting because when you take it, you are supporting a drug trade many thousands of miles away that destroys innocent people's lives. On a more prosaic level, cocaine is disgusting because, in your need for it, you can become the kind of person who might, while at the Notting Hill Carnival, be minded to go off with a strange man to a squat to score it, handing him fifty quid and leaving with a wrap that, when you go to open it when back at the party you are attending, you discover is completely empty.

Cocaine is disgusting because you will leave your friend's wedding and miss the apparently highly emotional speeches to wait for your dealer to turn up. Cocaine is disgusting because you will blow all your money on it and then you will have to call your unsuspecting mum and ask to borrow money while she is sitting at your grandmother's bedside in hospital. Cocaine is disgusting because one night you might go to meet your dealer and, just as you are about to reach his car, a police van pulls up and officers swoop on him and lead him away in handcuffs. Cocaine is disgusting because instead of seeing this as the close shave that it so clearly is, you will be annoyed that you have to spend a Friday night without any gear. But mostly, cocaine is disgusting for the way it makes you feel the next day, like a thousand tiny knives have shredded all your nerves into thin, brittle strips.

I'm making out that cocaine was to blame for all of this, when in actual fact the only person responsible was me. Also, in picking the most extreme moments of ten years I've made it sound really seedy, when quite often we would do nothing more outrageous than play Trivial Pursuit for so long that we would get back to the beginning of the questions and still not remember the answers because we were so fucked up. And when I say 'we', that is because I was not alone in my love of the drug. All around me were perfectly sane, functional human beings who liked nothing more than blowing the week away by getting on the chiz every Friday night. People who would never dream of drinking anything other than organic fairtrade coffee would happily shove illegal drugs harvested by impoverished small children up their hooters.

I always think that out there thousands if not millions of people have coke in their systems, and cocaine use is as endemic as drinking. But maybe I am mistaken. Maybe I think everyone takes cocaine because as my twenties tick by, I only ever really hang out with people who do. I am trying to make my world larger, more interesting, but in the process I only ever manage to make it smaller, really.

The popular image of a drug user is someone dirty, destitute, down and out. But when I look back at Facebook pictures from the time, I don't seem to be any of these things. I have glossy hair, good skin, slightly dilated pupils. I am smiling, slim, smoking, always with an arm thrown around someone or a piece of tinsel wrapped around me like a scarf. I don't look like a deranged lunatic with a drug habit. I look normal. I look like I am having a good time.

And sometimes I was. I really was. I have many happy memories that override the fact I was high on coke at the time, and make me forget the low points afterwards that weren't so much long, dark nights of the soul as long, dark mornings and days. Great parties. Great friends. Endless japes and anecdotes. This isn't something drugs campaigners will ever admit to, but you do have to be having a vaguely good time to keep going back to them. So this chapter isn't the story of my drugs hell. It is the story of my drugs limbo, a place I went to until I was fortunate enough to escape to somewhere much better, to the place I am now.

And now that I am an exhausted mother in my mid-thirties who has a hangover after half a bottle of wine, it's hard to remember how I managed to function at the time, how I managed to be both a successful career girl and someone with a drug habit. The truth is, I did some of my best work the morning after the night before. On a comedown, I had the pure focus to get things done so I could leave the office again. In many ways, I wasn't that different from the responsible parents who needed to get home to their little darlings. The difference was that my aim was to get home to some broccoli and an early night, so I could sleep off the excesses of the evening before.

And my aptitude for behaving like a tit and then telling people about all the ways I had behaved like a tit had some benefits. (I call it an aptitude because I am not entirely sure that it's a talent.) One of my editors picked up on it and suggested that I fill the confessional single girl about town column in the back of the Sunday supplement. So at least I put my wild ways to some sort of constructive use. At least it wasn't *all* in vain.

That's not to say I got away with it. I didn't always. I am not proud of any of the things that I am about to tell you but tell you I must. There was the time I had to cancel an important interview because I was still so out of it, pretending that my flat had flooded. I knew to email, rather than call, because at least then my boss wouldn't hear the alcohol in my voice. Once I went on Sky News to do the paper review still drunk. Nobody seemed to notice. Perhaps that's just how everybody does it. Then there was the night I went on such a bender that I managed to sleep until twelve, despite the fact it was column day and my deadline was 2 p.m. Somehow, I managed to get it done. I almost always managed to get it done. I worked hard and I played hard. Yes, I was always in the pub, but you could also always rely on me to write six pieces in a day before going back to sink another eighty-seven pints of lager, because what else did I have to do?

Did my colleagues know? I don't think they did. I could talk about all the crazy things I'd done on a night out except for the cocaine. That was the one secret I would happily keep close to my chest. Literally. (Sometimes, when partying, I would keep my wraps of coke in my bra, along with a card and a rolled-up note, so I didn't look suspicious every time I went to the loo, which was often.) I think, because I was always one of the youngest people at the paper, they thought I could keep going on nothing more than my youthful energy.

And what about my parents? Today I can discuss it with my mother but ten years ago she didn't know what cocaine was, much less how to spot the telltale signs that her daughter might be taking it. Besides, she and my father were carving out the next chapters of *their* lives, post-divorce, and I was a grown-up who had taken up more than enough of their attention as a child, one who seemed to be doing pretty well in her career, jetting off to Los Angeles to cover the Oscars

175

and meet Justin Timberlake and hang out with her teenage crush, Robbie Williams. You can't scrape someone off the floor if you never find them there. You can't stage an intervention if you have no idea what it is you're supposed to be intervening in. If it looks like a duck, swims like a duck and quacks like a duck, then it probably is a duck, unless of course it's a human pretending to be a duck because she is high on drugs.

I wonder, now, if it was coke I really loved or booze. Coke sharpens you up, brings you into the moment. It enables you to carry on drinking for longer. So maybe alcohol was actually my first love. Maybe I only ever took drugs so I could fill myself with more wine. I ruminate on this now every time I put my child to bed and one of the first things I do is go straight for the drinks cabinet or the corkscrew. Do I have a problem? Then the first sip slips down, and I say to myself you've seen off enough problems to keep this one for at least a little while longer.

8

I think I might need to do something different

Despite some of the best therapy money can buy, plus a great deal of the worst, and enough medication to make me rattle like a pharmaceutical dustbin in an earthquake, by the time my thirties roll around I am still behaving like a teenage me – only a bad version of teenage me, with more illegal drugs, fewer morals and bigger debts. Any adolescent dreams of being married with small children, a townhouse and a Chelsea tractor have been dashed. Worse, they have proved to be completely deluded. I haven't even managed to learn to drive, which, along with swimming, writing and reading, is a basic life skill. The closest I've come to it was that accidental call to the motorbike centre, but perhaps it is for the best that

I am not put in charge of one and a half tonnes of metal and petrol.

I am still living with my little sister, although we have now left the silverfish and graduated to a flat in Camden, joined by Steve, the male friend who will never be a boyfriend, and who my mother mistakenly thinks will be a calming influence on us. Well, on me. In reality, Steve is just as booze-soaked and chaotic as I am. It's just that because he happened to have been born with only the one X chromosome, his rampant party-going doesn't seem to matter. If anything, it's expected of him, because men must sow their wild oats while women must be virtuous and nice at all times, lest their wombs start to resemble the set of a desolate Western film, the only thing inside them being the tumbleweeds that blow bleakly from one empty fallopian tube to another. So Steve is frequently rewarded for his exploits – 'Woah, Steve, I can't believe you went out sixteen nights in a row. You deserve a medal!' – while I am told off for mine. They're not becoming in a woman. They're not ladylike.

(OK. So I am sort of rewarded by having a party-girl column in the back of a Sunday supplement, but I am pretty sure its purpose is to raise eyebrows rather than to have people pat me on the back, which, incidentally, is still wearing yesterday's frock.)

One night – well, one morning, really – Steve and I are in the process of completing yet another massive bender that will conclude just before my sister wakes up from an eight-hour stretch of restful sleep. We are in an illegal mini cab, returning from a series of Soho dive bars and Steve, in the infinite wisdom he seems to develop only after eight pints and umpteen shots of tequila, has decided to lecture me on my behaviour – the behaviour that is almost exactly identical to his.

'You know, if you carry on like this, it's going to take its toll,' he says, as if he hasn't just consumed a month's worth of alcohol units in one night. And I know that he isn't talking about the general 'you'. I know that he is talking about me. 'You're going to age badly, like a cheap wine from Aldi. You're going to get old.'

'We're all going to get old,' I snap. I feel strung out and brittle, my earlier sense of alcohol-induced euphoria now giving way to that unique sense of cold, sharp panic that comes with the prospect of a day at work on no sleep.

'Yeah, but YOU,' he says, jabbing me in the sides, 'YOU still look a bit young. You won't do for much longer if you keep on hammering it like this. You could be a great catch if you just calmed down a bit, you know. You're funny, clever, pretty, have a great job. It's just the raging drug habit that puts people off.'

'Why is it that, increasingly, the only compliments people pay me are backhanded ones?'

'Because they shcare about you,' slurs Steve.

'If you cared about me you would shut up.'

179

I'm staring out of the window at the breaking dawn, and the normal people who are already making their way to work. It's such a simple thing – getting up on time, without a hangover, eating breakfast, grabbing a coffee, reaching your desk with a smile on your face because you're not late. So why when I manage it does it feel like such a minor miracle? Why does being a normal, functioning member of the human race, like these people on the other side of the window, feel like such an impossibility? I feel the familiar sensation of a cocaine cry coming on, but stop it in its tracks.

'I really don't need to be lectured by you. I KNOW FULL WELL WHAT A FUCK-UP I AM.'

'Please, you no swear,' says the illegal mini-cab driver, who has had the moral high ground since the beginning of the journey. This is what my life has come to. I am actually being hectored on behaviour by a pissed man hurtling towards his forties and a stranger making a living illegally, who probably doesn't have a driving licence let alone a mini-cab one. I am being mansplained by people who don't have a clue. I apologise meekly and note that Steve has passed out. We eventually arrive home. Twenty-five-minute taxi journeys in the morning seem to take far longer than twenty-five-minute taxi journeys the night before, when you were high on drugs and cheap wine and all that mattered was your next hit.

I hand the driver the money and give Steve a long,

hard nudge. He comes round, and we make our way to the flat, where my sister is eating porridge and watching breakfast television. She doesn't say anything – she doesn't need to. The look on her face has enough contemptuous pity in it for a thousand nagging lectures. 'You know how Mum always said you would come into your own in your thirties?' mentions Naomi, when she finds me slumped at the bottom of the stairs with a bannister in my hand after a particularly heavy night out. 'Well, I think it might be wishful thinking, don't you?'

My thirtieth birthday party passes by in a blizzard. It takes place in July so you can guess what that blizzard mostly consists of. I have only the haziest of memories of the occasion, other than doing a line of cocaine off a car bonnet with a friend while we wait for my sister and Steve to get back from the off licence, because, naturally, I have forgotten my keys. They arrive just as the rest of the pub do. In one of many moments of madness that evening, pieced together only thanks to eyewitness reports from friends, I seem to have invited everyone back to ours, including the bar staff. It's gone midnight but I feel like the evening has only just begun. It could be 8 p.m. or 1 a.m. or 3 a.m. I am far too strung out to notice. At some point a neighbour comes down and threatens to kill us. At another, I apparently snog the bar manager, and some time in the late morning, my mother turns up unannounced bearing a lavish birthday cake and a look of horror on her face at our detritus-strewn flat – the overflowing makeshift ashtrays created out of the beautiful crockery she had bought us as a moving-in present; the half-drunk bottles of beer left not very strategically on shelves and toilet cisterns and worktops; the endless cracked CD cases that I can probably pass off as musical entertainment even though nobody has listened to a CD for five years, and certainly not one by New Kids on the Block. My mother puts us to bed and when we wake up the flat is spotless, and she has vanished. Not once do I think about how hard it must be for her to have such a screw-up of a daughter, how anxious and on edge she must always be, or at least, right now I don't. There will be plenty of time for this guilt in the future. Currently, I am just relieved to have got away with it. I just want to banish this hangover. I just want to be able to move on to the process of creating my next one. I just want to bury this feeling under some others.

If the definition of madness is doing the same thing again and again while hoping for a different result, then I am a complete fruitcake. Day after day, week after week, month after month and year after year, I repeat mistakes in the hope of a different outcome. Except, do I even know what I'm hoping for? Indeed, dare I even hope for anything at all? When I'm high, I have a habit of blathering on and on about the same thing, and when it comes to my more generalised behaviour, I am no different. I am a broken record that nobody wants to listen to – monotonous, tedious, tuneless. Here I am at thirty years of age and here are all the signs that I have not moved forwards. The signs are all there that I might have moved backwards, that I might have actually regressed.

I am still vomiting up my food sporadically. The reason I do it sporadically is because I barely eat anything other than a packet of Skips in the early evening to line my stomach before I start yet another bender. Cocaine has a way of suppressing the old appetite. I long ago stopped viewing bulimia as unhealthy and have even managed to convince myself that everyone does it from time to time. But twice a week? Yes, well. Let's gloss over that.

It is hardly surprising, then, that my scalp is still beset with bald patches. Fortunately, I have been simultaneously blessed with thick hair (the Lord works in mysterious ways) so with some nifty handiwork as I'm dashing out the door of a morning, I can usually cover them up. But one day, as I sit at my desk idly stalking some unsuspecting man on Facebook, a new colleague taps me on the shoulder. 'I just thought you should know that you have a patch of . . .' The new colleague becomes flustered and stumbles over his words. My brain races through all the patches I could have unwittingly been walking around with on me all day – a patch of spilt coffee, a patch of sick, or worse, a patch of semen? 'You've, you've got a patch on your head. No hair,' he finishes meekly, and the relief must come off me in waves.

'Oh, I know about that,' I say cheerfully, turning back to my stalking exercise. I pull my hair up in an attempt to cover the patch, and do not realise that at this point, my alopecia is literally the least weird thing about me.

With a coke habit and a love of alcohol, it will perhaps not be news to you that my OCD has now become a part of everyday behaviour. It's crept into my brain, set up home and put its feet up as the kettle boils, and all the while I've been too out of it even to notice.

I spend at least an hour of every day checking the sent items in my inbox for abusive messages my OCD suggests I might have sent to the editor, *and I do not think this is weird*. I return to the bathroom six times before I leave the office to check that I have not scrawled obscenities on the mirror, *and I do not think this is weird*. When replying to readers' letters at work, I ask the features desk manager to read the letter and check all over the envelope in case I have written that I am a child abuser, *and I do not think this is weird*. At home, when I have a drink, I have to ask Steve if he has seen me pour bleach in it, to which he replies, 'But Bryony, we don't have any bleach,' *and I do not think this is weird.* Some mornings, I take the iron to work in my handbag because that is just easier and more time efficient (if not energy efficient) than having to spend hours checking that it is properly switched off, *and I do not think this is weird.* And sometimes, when I am out drinking with friends and need to go to the toilet, I have to ask them how long I was gone to check that I haven't been raped in the loo, because, obviously, when someone replies, as they inevitably do, that I was 'only gone two or three minutes', I can reason that two or three minutes is not ample enough time for a sexual assault to take place, *and I do not think this is weird.*

I still see my reliance on antidepressants as a failure. Every pill I take is a symbol of what a fuck-up I am. It's as if I think mental illness is something that I might grow out of, like puppy fat or having an imaginary friend. I want to shake my thirty-year-old self by the shoulders and say, 'No, Bryony! OCD is not an imaginary friend. It is a very real enemy, and very real enemies do not just disappear if you ignore them, you blithering fucking IDIOT!'

I'm writing as if my life aged thirty is a complete and utter disaster, and yet it's not that bad. Professionally, things are going great guns. Somehow, miraculously, I am not screwing up my work, because at work, as with almost everywhere else that isn't the flat I live in, the

185

symptoms of my mental illness are seen as quirks of my personality, kooky affectations that make me really good fun to be around. The best! 'Hahahaha, that Bryony is just mad isn't she? Such a character!' Believe me. No single woman in her thirties wants to be described as a character. We should – it's good to be a character, much better than relying solely on your looks – but we don't.

Also, I may often be late, but I am willing to turn the reasons for my lateness into copy. I am willing to turn my disasters into words that other people would rather keep to themselves, because they have dignity and decorum and a sense of self-worth. Me? I think dignity and decorum are overrated, and that there is much more joy in making a tit of yourself and then writing about it, because if you laugh at yourself first, then it doesn't matter if anybody else does. You are owning your idiocy, if you will. (Although of course I don't write about the coke; even for me, that is an idiocy admission too far.) Plus, writing about all my failings will make people like me, I reason, because nobody likes a clever clogs, do they? I am a useful idiot, the one who makes you feel better about yourself.

My gobbiness has other advantages, too. I will ask outrageous questions in interviews because, hahaha-hahaha, aren't I funny. It is also often mistaken for a sign that I am opinionated, which eventually

– extraordinarily, some might say – lands me a column on the comment pages, where I can write down what I think about the news events of the week (as long as they are the fluffy news events of the week, involving either Kate Middleton or *Strictly Come Dancing* or the fact that the city of St Tropez has banned topless sunbathing). Actually, it is my experience that the most opinionated people are often the quietest, most thoughtful ones, but I am thankful that someone out there made an error of judgement one morning and asked me if I could bash out 600 words on something-or-other for the Notebook slot usually occupied by Andrew Marr's guinea pig (really – don't ask), because here I am all these years later, effectively doing the same, except in much longer form for way more money.

My promotion to columnist handily coincides with the birth of online comments. It's hard to believe that there was a time when these didn't exist, and there wasn't some arsehole buzzing in your ear all the time like a mosquito. Certainly, now I can't imagine writing without them. Every time my pieces appear online, the same people show up to offer their thoughts on my looks, on my gender, on my feminist agenda, which in most cases turns out to be evident for no other reason than that I am a woman. Perusing them, I have some idea of what it must be like to listen to me after a few lines of coke, going on and on and on as if anyone actually gives a shit. 'Don't read the comments!' my colleagues say, but are they mad? That would be like overhearing your name in another room and ignoring it. It would be like reading your own name on the boss's screen and not wanting to know more. Plus, they're never anything worse than I am actually thinking myself. They're never any match for the endless critics that have set up shop in my own head.

But I'm being negative again. There I am, with my fabulous job, moaning about the handful of sad men who still live with their mothers and spend their days wanking over newspaper websites; there I am, always with the miserable. And anyway, none of this really matters, does it? None of this really matters because there's something else I need to tell you. And what I need to tell you is this. Finally, remarkably, I seem to have a boyfriend.

As ever, this is not quite as straightforward as it might at first seem. When I say I have a boyfriend, what I actually mean is that I have a husband. And when I say I have a husband, what I actually mean is that I have someone else's husband. And when I say I have someone else's husband, what I actually mean is I am having an affair. A full-blown, low-down, dirty, disgusting affair. Yet another misshapen piece that will never fit the jigsaw puzzle in my mind.

I know, I know. It's as if I have a fucked-up bucket list I am going through with a fine-tooth comb. Drug habit? Check. Eating disorder? Check. Alopecia? Check. Divorced parents? Check. A handbag that contains an iron? Check. A man who is using you for sex and whom you are using for some screwed-up form of validation? Check, check, check.

I don't know how this happens, just as I'm not too sure how any of the other shit has happened. When I was a child, I had a pathological fear of my parents going off with other people, so it seems strange – almost deliberately nasty, even – that I might choose to visit one of my greatest worries on some other, innocent being. But then, from quite early on in my 'relationship' with this man, it is clear that he will not leave his wife, certainly not for me. So why did I do it, you must be thinking? Why did I bother? To this day, I have no answers, no excuses, only the vaguest sense that it must have been because I had absolutely no self-esteem and was desperate to be loved, even if it was by a man who sort-of-just-liked-me. In the grips of a drug habit, I was incapable of making any kind of moral judgement. But that doesn't make it OK, that doesn't make it better or justify my behaviour, and as I sit here writing this, it is still one of the things I feel most ashamed about.

I've read about women who go out of their way to pursue married men, because they like to be lavished with gifts while having the freedom to get on with their own lives. This is not me and I am doubtful if it is really, truly anyone, if they're being honest with themselves. Affairs are cruel, selfish, thoughtless things, and while I don't think I am cruel, I am, aged thirty, definitely selfish and thoughtless. Although I think all the time about myself, I am now at such a stage of self-absorption that I rarely take into consideration the feelings of anyone else, not my family, and certainly not his family.

I'll save you his name and the details of how we met, because these things do not matter and nor do they add anything to the well-trodden narrative of affairs that you have probably read about a thousand times before. He is confident, charming, blah blah blah, yada yada yada yada. My old friend hindsight suggests to me that I probably wasn't the only 'other' woman he had entertained, and that I possibly wasn't even the only one at the time.

I don't go looking for a married man but I don't exactly make it difficult for him to find me, and I don't go out of my way to tell him to clear off. Ludicrously, it doesn't even occur to me to suggest that he slings his hook. Nope. I will take any attention, however dubious, dangerous or undesirable it is. All the warning signs are there from the very beginning, flashing, screeching, telling me not to get involved, and yet I steadfastly ignore them in the deluded belief that this will be different, and love will conquer all. I have nothing to lose, and when you have nothing to lose, where's the harm? Plus, there are certain people who claim that they can have affairs without getting hurt, but were I to stop and think this through properly, I would see that the only person who wasn't going to get hurt was him, the man having his cake and eating it without so much as suffering a bout of indigestion.

We met just before my twenty-ninth birthday and for a while it was exciting, really it was. He was charming, erudite, so different from the men I was used to, who hung out in spit and sawdust pubs and didn't wash their hair for weeks. He took me to expensive restaurants and bars, and gave me the odd gift – a classic novel inscribed with a sweet message, a bunch of flowers delivered to my desk. Then, when he realised I was more of an open wound than a mistress, he stopped with the special attention. He didn't need to lavish it on me, didn't need to make any effort. Gosh, I bet he couldn't believe his luck – a twenty-nine-year-old with perky tits and only the loosest of morals, handing him everything on a plate. If he went quiet for a few days, he knew I would soon start begging to see him. If he turned up an hour late, he knew I wouldn't say a single thing, so desperate was I to see him. I was a needy, desperate husk. I actually thought I was in love with him, despite the fact he only ever paid me the most minuscule amount of attention possible. And that is not love, I now realise. It is self-loathing.

When I look back on this, it's almost amusing to think that I couldn't even manage to have an affair right. I mean, it would be amusing, were it not quite so pathetic. While other mistresses are busy being drenched in diamonds and designer handbags, I made do with the dregs of his time. An evening in a corporate hotel once a fortnight that we would go halves on despite him being far wealthier than I was; a few crappy texts telling me how sexy I was and how much he enjoyed shagging me. I told myself this was wonderfully naughty – I told myself a lot of things while I was not-really-with-him – and read the messages aloud to Chloe. But even she was appalled; even she could barely conceal her disgust.

Once he came round to my flat while Steve and my sister were out. It was a Saturday just before Christmas and he had with him a Fenwick bag that made me even more stupid with excitement. A lavish gift, for me! See, he does adore me! I had spent all afternoon cleaning our place until it shone in fear that a dirty hob or a stray pubic hair in a toilet might have him legging it for the door, as if he were going to be examining my worktops and not my boobs. By the time he arrived I was wearing stockings and suspenders, like some feeble impression of a French maid. He placed the Fenwick bag on the floor and then I let him take me over our dining table, which rarely saw any action other than this. I could see the turquoise blue of the bag shining out of the corner of my eye as he pummeled away at me, and then, like that, he was done, asking where the bathroom was and if I wouldn't mind if he had a shower before he left.

I got into the shower with him in a pathetic attempt at intimacy, but he looked kind of irritated – it wasn't a big shower, not the luxury rain shower model he probably had back in his giant, family home – and so I got out and went to get dressed. When he emerged, he thanked me for a wonderful afternoon, as if he had been at mine for longer than half an hour, and then he picked up the Fenwick bag, my heart fluttered, and he made for the door. 'Better get going,' he said. 'Need to deliver these gifts to the cleaner and the nanny.' That was where I ranked in his life – below the hired help.

Another time he told me he was going to a conference in Manchester, and asked me if I wanted to come for a night. I jumped at the chance, of course I did, but was slightly surprised when the day before no information on transport was forthcoming. 'Have you booked your train ticket, delicious one?' he texted that night, so off I went to the National Rail website where I paid £90, on top of the £200 I had already spent on Agent Provocateur underwear for the occasion, fully aware that he would not have splashed out on new boxers for me, and that his whole trip would be on expenses. When I arrived in Manchester, he told me he was still busy at the conference – of course he was – and to go to the hotel room, where I made myself uncomfortable in my corset and waited for him. A whole Friday night I spent in that soulless, corporate hotel room, by myself, speed drinking wine from the mini bar, waiting for him to let me know when he planned to show up. The hours ticked by, and no reply to my texts appeared. I started to wonder if I had got the wrong room, if some stranger was going to walk in at any given moment and scream at the sight of a trumped-up woman dressed like a sex worker. But company was wishful thinking, and while the rest of my friends were back in London, living it up on their Friday night as they should have been, I was alone in a strange city, wondering if it would be acceptable to start on the miniature bottles of spirits.

When he eventually turned up, just after 11 p.m., he was apologetic and complimentary about my corset. But he was also keen to watch *Newsnight*, and what's an important man with a piece of crumpet and an economic crisis to keep abreast of to do? Fuck the crumpet with one eye on the television, that's what. Have you ever tried having sex to the dulcet tones of Jeremy Paxman? Well look, I've done it for you, so you don't have to. You can thank me for it later.

I was a crappy person to have an affair with because my gobshite tendencies meant I told everyone, even my mother – who tells their mother they are having an affair? – who warned me it wouldn't end well and that I deserved better than this. But I didn't think I did. I honestly thought he deserved better than me, and that I was lucky he was deigning to spend what little time he did with me. I spent most waking hours, and some sleeping ones, too, worrying that my verbosity would cause him to leave me (as if he was even really 'with' me) and it never even once occurred to me that I should leave him. It genuinely didn't cross my mind. There weren't any other options open to me so why would I be so foolish as to jettison the one man who seemed to like me?

I excused my behaviour in all sorts of ways. I wasn't really the one in the wrong, was I, because I wasn't cheating on anyone? (I was, actually. I was cheating on myself.) Once I wrote a piece for a woman's magazine under a pseudonym in which I spouted forth for 1,500 words my theory that by having this affair, I was actually saving his marriage, because I was having the sex with him his wife didn't want. I think this goes some way to telling you how fucked up I was at this time. I actually believed I was doing her a favour by stabbing her in the back. I was so out of it I was incapable of rational thinking. I thought about her a lot, this mystery woman with whom he shared most of his life, with whom he had produced a gaggle of children and with whom he would get pregnant again, telling me one Valentine's Day. I painted an unflattering portrait of her in my mind, deciding she was boring and sexless, and that she was the one at fault, not me. I actually fantasised about her finding out and telling us we deserved each other and that she was through with him. That appalls me now. Of all the things I was doing when I turned thirty, it is the thing that makes me realise how low I went, how I plundered the very depths of morality. The truth is I knew nothing about this woman, and I am sorry if she ever knew about me. He only ever once mentioned her, and it was to tell me how much he loved her. How ironic it was that if we met, we'd probably really get on. He couldn't even bother to lie and tell me she didn't understand him. I wasn't worth the effort.

The incredible thing is that I actually told myself he was one of the good ones. He was better than Paul, I told myself. He was better than the men who shagged me once and then never had the decency to contact me again, I told myself. But actually, those men were far better, because they didn't keep me waiting. They didn't mess me about or string me along, despite me thinking that they had. They fucked me and left me, sure, but, in a way, that's more honourable than continuing to fuck someone you don't have to leave because you're not properly with them in the first place.

It's pointless, though, ranking the integrity of all the men I ever slept with. I chose them. I was the one whose behaviour was to blame.

At some point, even I have to say 'enough is enough' and that point is when *Private Eye*, a satirical current-affairs magazine, puts me in its 'Street of Shame', a sort of sin bin for badly behaved journalists. The gist of the piece is that I am having an affair with someone I shouldn't be (although I am not sure anyone has ever had an affair with someone they should be). It's my own fault. If you don't want to get caught doing something, then don't do it in the first place . . . but it still feels like a nadir has been reached. 'It's an honour,' says a well-meaning colleague of my appearance in the magazine, but it doesn't feel like one. I certainly don't plan on framing the piece and putting it in the loo for guests to see. And at the back of my mind there is always that critical voice, saying: 'Only you could go into journalism and somehow gain notoriety for your sex life rather than your work.'

When even Chloe is despairing of your behaviour, you know that something has to change and you have to do the thing you really don't want to do. 'But they don't understand that I LOVE HIM,' I wail, but I'm not even sure I'm convinced of this any more and I swear her eyes don't just roll out of her sockets but out of her actual head. It is the spring after my thirtieth birthday – the spring just after the Valentine's Day on which he chose to tell me his wife was pregnant again – and although I am still seeing him sporadically, like a junkie who can't break the habit, I know I don't want to feel this way any more. I know I don't want to feel desperate and grasping and empty. I know that this can't go on.

I am trying to write up an interview with Richard and Judy when my boss shouts over her desk and tells me she has a proposition for me. I know that her definition of a proposition is somewhat different from mine. It usually involves some sort of ritual humiliation, like dyeing my hair pink or spending a day getting shat on in the penguin enclosure at London Zoo. Don't get me wrong. I'm not complaining, for once. It's not as if I'm down a coal mine, is it? But every time she says these words, my stomach tightens slightly at what is coming, especially now, when I am already feeling like a prize tit. 'Let's humiliate Bryony,' I imagine her thinking. 'I'm not sure she's quite managed to do it enough herself.'

'So, Bryony Gordon,' says my boss, the fakest, most showbizzy of smiles on her face. 'Do you know what I think you need?'

I cast my mind over all the things I need – a proper boyfriend, some self-esteem, a detox.

'I think you need to spend two weeks travelling from Scotland to the Arctic Circle in a tiny speedboat with seven men you've never met before.'

Nope. That wasn't on my list.

'I what?'

'Nobody's ever done it before,' she says, as if this might somehow make the proposition more inviting.

'Maybe there's a reason nobody's ever done it before,' I say, panic rising in my oesophagus.

'I'm not going to send you on a job that's going to kill you, if that's what you're worried about.'

'It's just I don't know much about boats. I've been on a ferry and a pedalo and that's about it.'

'But haven't you always wanted to learn more about them?' she says, eyes sparkling with faux enthusiasm.

'Not really.'

'Look, why don't you think about it overnight? I think it will be a once-in-a-lifetime experience and you'd also get to be out of the office for two whole weeks. That's my idea of bliss, even if you would have to spend it on a tiny boat in choppy waters.'

'Maybe you should do it instead?'

'Think about it. Now go and finish Richard and Judy. You're already an hour late filing.'

So I do what she says. I finish Richard and Judy, and then I take the bus to the King's Road to buy a dress I do not need and cannot afford and only want because it showcases my tits spectacularly and there is still a pathetic, gnawing part of me that wants to impress the man-who-is-not-a-boyfriend-but-somebody-else's-husband. In the fitting room, my phone rings. It is a man called Hugo who is organising the trip to the Arctic Circle, wanting to sound me out and tell me what it will involve. I am holding the dress in one hand and the phone in the other as he details the journey – in a rigid inflatable boat (no idea), across the entire bloody North Sea in one twelve-hour crossing, up the coast of Norway, before arriving in the Arctic Circle on a date that happens to be my thirty-first birthday, seeing whales and dolphins and seals as we go – and as he goes on, something inside of me clicks. Maybe it's the mention of my birthday, which seems like some kind of sign, or maybe it's the mention of the whales and dolphins and seals, but somehow I find myself saying yes to Hugo. 'Go on then, I'll do it,' I say, and then I buy the dress on autopilot, leave the shop, and go home and tell my sister and Steve what I have done.

'You're mad,' is the general consensus.

'You can't even drive a car, let alone a boat,' says Steve.

'Your hair will get wet,' says my sister.

'You'll moan about the cold,' continues Steve.

'You might get eaten by a polar bear,' nods my sister. And so on and so on.

But polar bears are the least of my worries right now. In my bedroom, the dress glitters at me shallowly and I realise it is a kind of symbol of why I have to do this trip – because my life now has a shameful monotony to it that needs to be broken. Dresses I don't need, men I don't need, drugs and alcohol I don't need . . . Two weeks in a boat might not be enough to break the monotony, but it is certainly a start. It is something.

'Also, one of the seven men might be the love of your life,' says Chloe, and I have to say that the thought had crossed my mind. 'Imagine the story you could tell the grandkids – we met on a glorified dinghy in the North Sea.'

A glorified dinghy is exactly what a rigid inflatable boat is, as it turns out.

'Where are we going to sleep?' I ask Hugo.

'In youth hostels.'

I can feel the bed bugs biting me already.

'And where's the toilet?'

'The sea,' says Hugo, simply, and it's OK for him and the rest of the men on this trip, but what about me with my delicate lady anatomy?

I am bricking it by the time the trip rolls around. A day on a rigid inflatable boat (RIB for short), in the Solent with Hugo has done nothing to allay my fears. Although these boats are small, they can travel at a rate of more than 30 knots. When the sea is calm, this is fine, and the RIB skims the surface of the water smoothly, but any change and it actually jumps out of the water, slamming back down with an almighty thud that leaves your tummy in your mouth and your bones rattling as you cling on for dear life.

'They do capsize,' explains Hugo, calmly, as if this is just fine. 'They sort of flip over if the waves get too big.'

'Don't tell me that,' I snap, and in my head *The Perfect Storm* is playing out, only without George Clooney and Mark Wahlberg.

I meet everyone else for the first time at Edinburgh airport. There is Julian, a self-confessed musician and 'speed freak'; Paul, who had designed, built and tested RIBS 'in the most severe conditions' – gulp; Andy, who liked nothing more than taking his kayak out on the sea for miles and miles every weekend; Mark, a former member of the armed forces, who was now an engineer; Ed, a photographer who liked going on adventures; and Pete, a seasoned sailor who had once won the Légion d'honneur for sailing into a hurricane to save a French sailor, while taking part in a solo round-the-world race.

I know what you're thinking. You're thinking, 'Do you fancy any of them?' The answer is no, but God, I do love all of them. They are decent and funny and good and to them I am a rounded human being rather than a piece of meat. None of them know what a fuck-up I am. It's as if I'm wiping the slate clean and starting again. I'm finding a new me, one who can withstand the elements without collapsing and crawling to the off licence before calling a dealer.

We fly from Edinburgh to Wick, a town in the far north of mainland Scotland, in a tiny propeller plane, and although we are ricocheted around like pinballs in an arcade machine, my fear of flying seems to have evaporated (as it did in Virgin's upper class under totally different circumstances) – or at the very least been replaced by a much bigger sense of dread about what is in store over the next two weeks and 1,000 nautical miles.

In Wick, we go straight to the harbour, where in a cold, grey office on a cold, grey June day, Hugo hands us all our kit and the enormity of what we are doing really begins to sink in.

Any desperate delusions that we will be lounging about in deck shoes, shorts and polo shirts are soon shattered by the helmets Hugo hands us all. Actual, proper helmets. The uniform is far more technical and a lot less flattering than I had imagined. There are thermal tops and leggings, salopettes as if we are about to go skiing, a waterproof jacket, a fleece to go under the waterproof jacket and finally, crucially, a bright yellow dry suit, £1,000 worth of thermal protection should the boat end up capsizing us into the water.

'These are sometimes used to protect workers from hazardous materials,' explains Hugo cheerfully. 'Fall in with one of these on and you'll most likely float, so there's nothing really to worry about.'

'Most likely?' I bleat, tucking my helmet underneath my arm. 'Nothing really?'

The men start changing into their uniforms so I slink off to the toilet, where I realise that going to the loo is not going to be the problem – getting in and out of the suit is. This is an ordeal in itself, and if I can't even dress myself without bursting into tears, what hope do

I have of making it all the way to the Arctic Circle in a souped-up skiff? What am I doing here? Am I even here at all, or is this all some strange, surreal dream? And have I lost the plot completely?

It takes me half an hour to wrestle my boobs and hips and curvy lady bits into the umpteen layers of high-tech sailing gear, and when I look in the mirror, I realise I look like a DayGlo Michelin Man. I look like an extra from *2001: A Space Odyssey*. But it's time to get over myself. Lipstick, heels and tit-busting dresses don't mean jack-diddly-squat here. All that matters is that my bladder holds firm and the Imodium kicks in.

We dispense our belongings into waterproof backpacks and I note that while mine contains mascara, Touche Eclat and Agent Provocateur bras, the rest of the crew seem to have brought three T-shirts and five pairs of boxer shorts between them. On the crossing to the Shetland Islands I have to ask Hugo to stop the RIB so I can be sick over one side. As I finish my ablutions, a seal pops up and gives me a completely understandable look of contempt that makes me laugh even though I have flecks of regurgitated food on my face.

We are off the coast of Fair Isle. 'Are you OK?' Hugo shouts, but my weakness doesn't bother me one bit. I put my hand in the cold water and swirl it around to push my mess away from the seal, and as I do this the sun starts to shine bright in the sky and it occurs to me how nice it is to be sick without having to force myself; how strangely pleasant it feels for my body to behave naturally.

I splash some of the North Sea onto my face and then I feel the warmth of the sun on my cheeks as I watch the gannets and gulls swoop down from the cliffs and low over the boat, like dandelion seeds in the wind. But there is no breeze now – just summery, Scottish heat that paints everything beautiful and surprises me after the greyness of Wick; surprises me and makes me long to be off the boat. 'If we go in with the dry suits on, we won't ruin them, right?' I say to my fellow crew members, but I know the answer and before anyone else has had a chance to respond I am jumping over the side and into the North Sea, icy even in June. In the distance I see a cave and swim towards it, noting that behind me the rest of the crew have jumped over, too – because anything a girl can do they can do better. I reach the cave, come face to face with a family of puffins, say hello to them, then swim into the inky blackness, where nobody can get me and nobody but the puffins can see me cry my never-before-cried tears of joy.

This is the best decision I ever made, I think that night when I fall asleep in our B&B at 8.30 p.m., delirious from fresh air and exercise. We have to be up at 6 a.m.

to make the long crossing to Norway, but when I go down at the crack of dawn, bright-eyed and bushy tailed, I am told it is momentarily off due to bad weather. I feel nervous again, agitated. We go to the Viking museum – these are the only other people mad enough to have made such a crossing in a similar sized boat – and have fish and chips. Then at 3 p.m., we get the call. We are good to go in an hour. 'But that's overnight,' I squeal fearfully, but of course it doesn't matter, because we are now in the land of the midnight sun.

At 12 a.m., we stop the engines and jump into the North Sea, where in the background oil rigs twinkle like Christmas trees. At 1 a.m. I ask the boys to close their eyes as nature has called and I need to go off the back of the boat. The rigmarole surrounding this is not embarrassing, but liberating. If I can pee off the back of a tiny boat in the middle of the North Sea, I can do anything, right? A four-hour sunset bleeds into a magnificent sunrise, which bathes everything in pink. Norway appears to us in the shape of tree-lined cliffs covered in waterfalls. When we arrive into port, we have a celebratory beer before turning in for two hours' kip and the start of the next leg.

When we wake up, the weather has changed. The air smells fresh like pine needles and we will be motoring through fjords, but we cannot really see the hills on either side of us, which have been shrouded in fog. The wind stings my face but at least hides my pathetic, fatigued tears as the boat jumps eight foot out of the water. I get so sick and so shivery that I manage to fall asleep next to an engine while the rain hammers down on me. By the end of the day my body aches from clinging to the boat, but I still know I have made the right decision and that the pain is good. The aching is a sign of my body getting strong. It is a sign of my body getting better.

For the rest of the trip, the weather is glorious. We see golden eagles and bright purple jellyfish that float in the turquoise waters. I am covered in blisters and have started my period and haven't looked in a mirror for a week but I couldn't care less. 'You're a gutsy bird, Bryony,' one of my boat boys tells me the night before we arrive in the Arctic Circle – the night before my birthday – and when it turns midnight in the blazing sunshine, they present me with a cake and candles that have been transported all the way from Scotland.

My thirty-first birthday is the first for a decade that I remember with clarity, the first that doesn't pass in a haze of excessive self-abuse. A year before I was snorting lines of coke off car bonnets, but now I am arriving in Svolvær, a beautiful town in the untouched land of the Lofoten Islands, about 170 km above the start of the Arctic Circle. It is surrounded by snow-capped mountains yet drenched in sun, 26 degrees day and night. 'We've got a treat for you,' says Hugo, and so it is that I find myself on the morning of my birthday, being taken to a faraway fjord where we watch a pod of killer whales swim around us for hours. I have tears in my eyes, but they are very different from those of twelve months ago, when my mother turned up unannounced in a flat full of cigarette ends and drug paraphernalia.

If she could see me now, she'd be happy. If she could see me now, she'd know that everything was going to be OK, even if I'm not entirely convinced of the fact. I turn on my phone for the first time in two weeks. No messages from him, but a zillion birthday texts from people who actually care. I call my mother and tell her everything I have done, all I have seen, and she sounds so relieved, so happy.

'I love you, Mum,' I say, for the first time in, what? Three years? Four years? Five?

'I've always loved you, Bryony,' she says.

We sail to an untouched beach in the shadow of a glacier, and there we have a picnic. Later, I creep off to take a loo break, the rigmarole of removing the dry suit and the salopettes now second nature to me, like so many things that were alien to me just a fortnight ago – not washing or wearing any make-up or taking drugs or obsessing about a morally bankrupt loser. Everyone has to take control of their lives at some point, I think, staring at a golden eagle that is dancing over the crest of the glacier. Everyone has the power to change things. And in the shadow of that glacier, while changing a tampon, I make the decision to do just that.

9

I think I might *actually* be in love

My old friend hindsight wants me to believe that what happens next would have happened anyway, that I am no more the mistress of my own destiny than I am likely to star in a movie with Brad Pitt and David Duchovny. Hindsight doesn't want me to take credit for the miracle that is to come. Hindsight wants me only to feel pathetic gratitude that somebody decent deigned to pick me out of the gutter, dust me down and walk off into the sunset with me, without me managing to fall into a pothole in the process. (I did once fall down a hole while 'pulling' someone, as it was known back when I was fifteen. I'd gone to a house party and crept off into the garden for a snog with a boy called Alex, who thought it would be better if we did what we had to do out of anyone's line of vision, because obviously it was only acceptable to pull monobrowed me in the pitch black where nobody could see. Sadly, I did not know that part of the lawn was in the process of being dug up to create a pond, and so it was that I found myself at the bottom of a six-foot hole covered in soil, as Alex sniggered from the top, not even bothering to try to haul me out. Bad choices, people. I've always made bad choices. Until now.)

But I'm beginning to think that hindsight is actually more of a foe due to his habit of making me feel like an arse. I'd like to think that I had *something* to do with the next chapter of my life, and my actions have not been responsible just for a catalogue of errors, fuck-ups and misunderstandings. I'd like to think that what happened next wouldn't have happened without the tiniest, weeniest input from me.

His name is Harry. Oh, I know what you're thinking. 'Let me guess, it's all made better by a man. How predictable! How depressingly, unoriginally predictable! Over 150 years of feminism we've had, and in one sentence you've just managed to shove us back into the kitchen, where we are on our knees giving some bloke a blow job while keeping one eye on the hob.' But I'm not suggesting for one minute that *your* life could be made better by a man. You might be a lesbian, for a start, or a straight male, in which case a man is unlikely to help matters. Also, it doesn't have to be a romantic companion that makes your life better. It could be a pet or a sport or meditation or painting. It could be morris dancing or alpaca farming. It could be cheese rolling or bog snorkelling. You know. Whatever floats your boat.

But if you are a heterosexual female (or a gay bloke) on the lookout for a life partner, I do not see what is wrong with thinking that life might be made better by finding one. It's not a betrayal of the sisterhood or a slap in the face of feminism, and nor should anyone make you feel that it is. People who do this tend to be self-righteous dicks who should really be focusing on the bigger picture – violence against women, for example, or the continued practice of female genital mutilation on marginalised women in Africa and the Middle East and the very country we live in. But criticising someone for craving companionship? It's like wishing you'd never been born – a total waste of time and energy, and you're not helping anyone when you do it. It's OK to want companionship. It's OK to want to be with someone. It's more than OK, actually, it's biology. It's the reason the human race has been so damn dominant as a species, and if you want to knock it on the grounds of setting back social justice, well then, more fool you. Do you think Emmeline Pankhurst or Gloria Steinem or Hillary Clinton or Lena Dunham would exist were it not for their mothers seeking out a warm man on a cold winter's night? No. No they wouldn't.

I'm not saying that the moment I found Harry, I immediately got better and it was as if the previous fifteen or so years of my life had never happened. As you will soon see, that is absolutely not the case. Plus, it's important here to make the point that in Harry, I did not seek out just any man. I didn't glance at the first bloke I saw across a room and think, 'He'll do, let's settle for this one.' I had actually known him for a couple of years, on account of the fact we both worked at the *Telegraph* and he was friends with Steve, but I'd never shown any interest in him and he had never shown any interest in me, other than expressions of mild contempt bordering on pity.

He is the banking correspondent, which officially makes him the least likely person at the *Telegraph* for me to get together with. I mean, I am more likely to get it on with the guy on security or the beauty columnist than a man who is so fascinated by finance that he has actually made it his career – worse than that, a career in finance that doesn't actually pay anything.

He is handsome, I'll give him that, but in a clean cut, posh way, and I imagine that at the weekends he wears red socks and loafers and can be found braying like a donkey in pubs on the King's Road. In the office he sort of nods at me when we pass in the corridor, as if to say, 'Oh yeah, you,' and when he comes round to the flat, he just sits there quietly in the corner as if judging me for my myriad fuck-ups. He's not for me, Harry. I am the spice to his sugar, the chalk to his cheese. I dismiss him as ordinary, make little or no effort to prove myself wrong, and at one point I even use the words 'sanctimonious' and 'toss bag' when describing him to his best pal, Steve, because people like him make me feel like a screw-up, even if they don't mean to at all and it's just me projecting my insecurities on to someone completely innocent.

'You mean he doesn't feel the need to behave like a prick all the time to get your attention?' says Steve.

'Whatevs,' I sulk.

Things start changing before my life-altering trip to the Arctic Circle, not that I have the wherewithal to notice this is the case (OK, hindsight is perhaps helpful on this count, but this count only). It's on Valentine's Day, ironically, that I first see the kindness behind Harry's brisk, boarding-school front, presumably built up after years of beatings from repressed homosexuals in ice-cold shower blocks. I have fled from the bar where the man-I-am-deluded-enough-to-think-I-love has informed me that his wife is pregnant. I have gone to an anti-Valentine's party where Chloe is 'celebrating' being single. I have got so drunk that I have fallen into a cab. I have got so drunk that I have left my debit card behind the bar, and although I am somehow able to retrieve my address from the darkest recesses of my mind, the same cannot be said of the details of where my cash card might be. I have arrived home, pissed, tearful and pursued by an angry taxi driver, and I have been ushered in through the front door by Steve, who tells me to sit in the living room while he goes to sort out my fare. And once in the living room, I have been confronted by Harry, who, instead of sneering at me like the pathetic loser at the bottom of a hole I so clearly am, comforts me, crossing the room to the sofa I have slumped on and placing an arm around my shoulder as I weep into his pin-striped shirt. It's always about me.

'You know what?' he says, as my mascara flows liberally over his crisply ironed top. 'You are wonderful, you really are. Any man would be lucky to have you. And it's about time you realised it.'

Yet still I do not see that Harry's contempt is actually confused curiosity, that the reason he is standoffish with me isn't down to dislike . . . it's simply because he doesn't understand how I could dislike myself so much. Nevertheless, his kindness that evening sticks with me. It creates a faint line of something – I am not quite sure what – that I dare not try to erase. I start to make more of an effort with him, like a teenager resolving to be nicer to their best friend's douchebag boyfriend. I join him and Steve on trips to the pub, don't strop off to my bedroom when he comes round, and even start going for coffees with him at

Pret A Manger during our breaks at work. Is this the true sign that something is changing? Would this be the bit in the montage part of the movie of my life where the audience realises that maybe, just maybe, everything is going to turn out OK? Is he the man who's been right under my nose all the time, the one I promised you wouldn't appear in this book? Is he the person we all mistakenly believed Steve to be?

Harry has always been there in the background but only now I have returned from the Arctic Circle does he start to emerge properly from the shadows; only now do I find myself going out of my way to make him laugh; only now do I brush my hair when he comes round; and only now does my stomach flip when a chat message from him springs up on my computer at work – chat messages that I go out of my way to close every time Steve hovers into view, because what if, what if, what *if*?

And only now do I feel proper contempt for the man I have been having an affair with. Only now do I find myself completely impervious to his messages, which of course have become more frenzied now that I have made the decision to shut him out of my life. And so it's only now that I feel able to tell hindsight to fuck off. I've had it with hindsight, the know-it-all so-and-so. Hindsight wants me to think I whistled into this one by the skin of my teeth, and should feel insanely lucky for what I've managed to achieve, be it in my personal life or my professional one. It wants to tell me that I could still lose it all tomorrow if I'm not careful, and it's not the only one. Last year, I received a Facebook message from an old school 'friend' who wanted to tell me how blessed I was to have secured such a decent, caring person in my life, how fortunate I should feel for this crazy turn of events, as if somehow I hadn't deserved them, and my outcome was not the correct and proper one for a screwed-up loon with substance-abuse problems and loose morals. That's the perceived, generalised wisdom out there. Girls like me don't deserve happiness. They don't deserve happy endings, or as I call what happened next, a happy beginning.

And maybe I did get lucky. Maybe my tale is all a crazy, fortunate fluke and I shouldn't be retelling it as if anything can be learnt from it, but something tells me otherwise. Harry was there when I was twenty-nine and he was there when I was thirty, and yet only when I was thirty-one, after my amazing tampon epiphany, did he start to make sense. Only when I started to believe that I deserved something more than misery did I get something more than misery.

This is why I'm harping on like a deranged preacher, because I do think I turned things around. And I firmly believe that if I can turn things around, *anyone* can. I don't think that my story has anything to do with luck; nor do I think people should be blasé about the positive things they've managed to achieve. I'm just saying that, for once, I feel a sense of pride that I made a decision to take some responsibility for my actions instead of hiding behind them, hoping that the world would one day deliver me a break. I'm proud I've finally realised that, actually, the only person who has ever been able to deliver me a break is, um, me.

Which, by the way, is not the same as pulling yourself together, whatever the naysayers might want you to think. It's not *at all*.

Harry does a note-perfect impression of Donald Duck, which for a moment makes all the bad things in the world go away. He shares a flat in south London with two old friends. It is strangely clean because he's not too keen on mess. In his bedroom, hidden in the bookcase, is a Snoopy dressed in cricket whites that makes my heart ache. He doesn't use deodorant but that doesn't bother me; ditto his toe nails which are . . . I mean, I don't even want to go there. He thinks Arnold Schwarzenegger is a genius and has a love of sci-fi that I appreciate. Like me, he knows a lot about *Star Wars*, but can take or leave the prequels. He likes a drink but doesn't take drugs because they give him panic attacks. He doesn't really smoke unless he is completely blotto when he is not averse to scabbing off me.

Harry is left-handed, which isn't that odd, and owns

a pink jumper that he loves more than any other item in his wardrobe, which is. He is a Gemini, a month and three days older than I am, and has a quiff that makes him look much younger. He has a pair of pyjama bottoms he wears every night to bed, and some trainers he will not part with even though they look like clown shoes. His voice gets deeper when he is talking to men he thinks are macho, an affectation I find incredibly sweet in its girlyness. He dreams a lot about his first pet, a golden labrador called Tug, and at night when he is tired, he likes to twirl my hair around his index finger. We have our first kiss in the garden of his flat in August of 2011. A month later he flies back early from a lads' holiday to Morocco (who goes on a lads' holiday to Morocco, I ask you?) and turns up at my door late one night straight from the airport to surprise me. 'He flew back for ME!!!' I text Chloe, momentarily throwing aside any concern for correct use of punctuation.

'Bloody hell,' she replies. 'It must be love. Either that, or it was a really crap holiday.'

Reader, I choose to believe the former.

He could not be more different from me. He is calm whereas I am choppy and changeable. He does not emote, whereas that is all I ever do. He is an only child and yet consistently unselfish – I am one of three and only seem to think about myself. He is the son of a colonel and grew up on army bases around Germany.

His mother died of breast cancer when he was in his early twenties, a fact he barely mentions because it obviously hurts him too much. Can you imagine if one of my parents had died instead of just getting divorced? You'd never have heard the end of it. We wouldn't have got past chapter four.

Our differences are so stark that people cannot fail to pick up on them. 'Poor Harry,' mutters Chloe after her first meeting with him. 'What has he let himself in for?' My sister is a little more blunt. 'He clearly really likes you, but I can't for the life of me understand why.' Yet those contrasts seem to be the very things that glue us together. He gives me a much-needed, content stability, while I draw things out of him he hasn't dared to air for years. From time to time it amuses me that I have fallen in love with someone from a military background, but later I will interview Ruby Wax, herself married to the son of an army colonel, and she tells me that chaos is what these men are used to. 'Dealing with us is probably like going into war.' She's joking, of course, but as with all the best jokes, it contains more than a grain of truth.

And of course I am fearful his father will disapprove, but he couldn't be more charming. The very fact I am introduced to him is a wonder in itself. After all this time in dysfunctional relationships that weren't even really relationships, meeting someone's family is not a dream I have ever dared to have. Even my mother is in shock. When I tell her that I have an actual boyfriend, and that I will be bringing him round for Sunday lunch, she almost faints, as if I have told her I have won the lottery or am planning on having a sex change, both of which must have seemed more likely at certain stages of my twenties.

It creeps up on both of us completely unexpectedly. You think you're going to be hit by a thunderbolt when it happens. You think that an orchestra is going to be playing in the background, and everything around you is going to fall away or freeze in time. Actually, no music plays, the world carries on as normal, and it's more a slow warm front coming in than any kind of freak weather condition – a warm front that has come about so gradually that you've not really noticed it before, but now that you have, goodness, isn't it wonderful? It's like waking up in leisurely fashion after a long winter, thawing out over a long period of time. And before you know it, you're drunkenly telling each other you love each other. Before you know it, you're making holiday plans. Before you know it, you're moving into his flat. Before you know it . . . well, I don't want to get ahead of myself. I don't want to curse this one before we've even properly got started.

Harry does not cure my OCD. He does not make my alopecia go away – well not directly, anyway. But the stability and contentment that suddenly appear in my life have a calming effect on me, even though it would be fair to say that getting into a relationship that is decent and good is new to me, and I have absolutely no idea how to behave. I am like a lifer let out of prison after thirty years. I am a desert-island castaway complete with full beard who has been rescued after a decade spent living in the wilds with only a volleyball for company. I may have managed to keep myself alive all that time, but I'm buggered if I remember how to do conversation. I'm socially inept, incapable of acting properly. I am having to learn a whole new set of mores. It's not so much that I've forgotten them – it's that I never knew they existed in the first place.

It's like watching Crocodile Dundee try to make it in the big city, or ET dressed up as a girl. I am a thirty-one-year-old writer at the *Daily Telegraph* with an expensive education behind me, and yet I do not seem to know how to act like an adult. For example, I do not know that it is not OK to turn up drunk at someone's house when that person has told you he's getting an early night because he has to be up at the crack of dawn to go to a family event. I do not know that it is not OK to work yourself into a state of paranoia so frenzied and inebriated that you convince yourself your other half is actually lying, when you have absolutely no evidence for that to be the case. I do not know that it is not OK to mistakenly knock on his neighbour's door at gone midnight, and I do not know that it is not OK then to pass out in your beloved's bed where you snore so loudly he gets no sleep, has to resort to ear plugs, and the next morning manages to destroy one of the mirrors of his car in an accident he swears is down to exhaustion.

I do not know that it is not OK to invite your other half to a big family get-together, and then, as everyone – cousins, aunts, uncles included – sits down for lunch, announce to the table that you have some news. 'We haven't got engaged,' you say, cracking a joke that I do not know will make everyone but my boyfriend laugh.

And I do not know that it is not OK to sit your other half down one evening and tell him everything terrible you have ever done, so that he is fully aware of what he is taking on and so you do not feel at any point that you are misleading him. I do not know that shame does not have to be shared, divided up into smaller parts so that other people get to feel it also. I do not know how to let things go, how to move on from the past and not burden everyone else with it, too.

It is a November night and the guilt I feel about my cocaine-induced behaviour is weighing heavily on me, like wet washing. It has been worrying me, bothering me for weeks. You could say I have been somewhat obsessing over it. Everything is going so well, everything is going so swimmingly, that there has to be a catch, hasn't there? And that catch is this. Harry cannot possibly know the full extent of what a fuck-up I am. He can't, because if he did, he would not be here with me right now, watching box sets and eating some terrible cous cous recipe we have knocked together. I need to tell him. I need him to know that it is not normal for me to be watching box sets and knocking together terrible cous cous recipes. I need him to know that I am damaged goods. I need him to know exactly the kind of person he is climbing into bed with every night before everything gets too far along and I unwittingly begin to deceive him. I need to do this because my OCD is telling me I have to. It's telling me I need to seek his reassurance, and that I would be an even worse person if I didn't.

'So there's something I need to tell you,' I say to him as one episode of *The Killing* ends, before he has a chance to start another.

'Right,' he smiles, no clue of what is coming next, of the monster he has been sleeping with for months. And then I tell him everything.

I tell him about every person I have ever slept with, about the burst wart and the abusive boyfriend and, most importantly, the obsessive compulsive disorder. I tell him that it's not like the OCD everyone jokes about. I don't have the good, cleaning-up type, and actually, there is no good type, the word 'disorder' being a clue to how horrible it is. I tell him I have the I-think-I-killed-someone type, the I'm-scared-I-will-turn-into-a-child-molester type. How I get the words out of my mouth, I have no idea but it feels weirdly good when I do, like opening a blocked valve or going for a piss having been deprived of a loo for six hours.

'Shh, stop,' says Harry, moving towards me on the sofa and putting his hands over mine. 'It's OK,' he says, and I cannot quite believe what I am hearing, cannot quite believe that I have stumbled upon such a decent human being. 'None of this matters. It really doesn't. It's your past, and everyone has a past. I mean, mine isn't quite as adventurous as yours but that doesn't mean to say I'm bothered by what you've got up to. Do you honestly think, every time I came round to your flat to see Steve, I didn't realise you were a bit out there and suffering from some kind of mental-health issue? Do you honestly think I've mistaken you for some kind of wallflower? Do you honestly think I care, or would be here if I didn't really, really like you? You've got to stop thinking you're a bad person, Bryony, because you're not. You've just made bad choices. That's all.' He pulls me into his neck and I breathe him in while letting some of my shame out.

For so long, I thought he was ordinary. Now I know he is actually extraordinary. He does not judge. He does not criticise, or question. Forgiveness washes off him in waves. Now I just have to learn how to forgive myself.

But I am making progress.

For all of my adult life, and a great deal of my

non-adult life, too, the worst thing you could have called me was 'fat'. Fat was the enemy, fat showed a lack of control, fat was the fate worse than death that I feared so much I would make myself sick every time I ate. But now fat attaches itself to me without me even noticing. One pound, two pounds, fourteen pounds. There aren't any scales at Harry's place, so it's only when I move up a dress size and then another that I realise I am becoming the thing I have always feared the most . . . and what's more, I don't seem to care.

I know piling on the pounds in the early stages of a relationship is somewhat of a cliché, but truth be told, I'm loving being a cliché. A stereotype. Part of a boring, dull couple who gaze into one another's eyes while living in a bubble of sex, wine and Chinese takeaway. Clichés have long been so bizarre to me that I can't help but rush to embrace them wholeheartedly now they are here – holding hands while walking through the park; lying in bed on Sunday reading the papers; smooching on a packed, rush-hour tube on the way to work.

A year ago, a size 16 would have appalled me, literally made me run to the loo to be sick. Now it seems to make perfect sense to me, even if it doesn't to everyone else. The first time anyone mentions it is below the line on an article I have written about an etiquette class I have been asked to report on. The piece is accompanied by pictures of me sitting with my legs folded correctly so as not to flash my knickers, standing with a book on my head and getting out of a car in a prim and proper way.

I'm looking at the pictures now, and I think I look great – far better than when I was skinny and empty and lacking even basic sustenance. But the men commenting on the piece do not agree. 'You've piled on the pounds,' says one. 'With the utmost respect, it's time to lose some weight,' writes someone else. And on and on the comments go, a reminder of the bile I used to taste daily when I was making myself sick all the time. 'I'd say these comments were close to the bone,' posts some hilarious joker, 'but in Bryony's case that seems to be slightly optimistic.'

It's one thing when a bunch of strangers vent abuse at you underneath a piece about etiquette, of all things; quite another when your friends start to comment. I'm at a bar with Chloe and some of our friends when one of them takes it upon himself to mention my new, fuller figure.

'You look different,' he says, clinging to a cocktail. 'You look, how can I put it? Well.'

The others snigger. Chloe snaps at him, tells him to be quiet, because we both know that this isn't meant as a compliment. We both know that looking well is a euphemism for piling on the pounds. But I'm done with living in a twisted world where looking gaunt and ill is celebrated. I'm done with treating myself badly in order to make myself look good.

227

Mad Girl

This is the truth of my weight gain. When you stop taking cocaine, start eating three meals a day and stop bringing up your food, your body has a way of recalibrating itself. The edges come off you, the ones that have made you spiky for so long. Your skin plumps out and dimples in places you once wouldn't have wanted it to. But your eyes get clearer, sparklier, and you realise that suddenly, after all this time of trying to look like someone else, you are starting to look like you. Not so weirdly, your alopecia patches begin to get smaller. And as you get bigger, something strange happens, something so unlikely that it appears to be a dream. You miraculously shed your skin of self-consciousness. You feel larger but better; you feel larger but stronger. And so parading naked in front of your boyfriend doesn't bother you. You don't mind so much that your tits sag without a bra on. You don't feel the need always to trump yourself up in scaffolded underwear to try to impress a man. You know that you are enough because you are more solid, not just in your body but your mind. You are literally more full of life. Your body is healing itself. And the thing that you have feared most for so many years is, you are slowly discovering, actually the best thing that will ever happen to you.

A year after Harry and I get together, I am dispatched to cover the London Olympics. The two are not linked in any way – such is the security surrounding major international sporting events in which over 10,000 athletes from over 200 countries take part, all the paperwork has to be sorted out years in advance – but they will eventually become forever linked in my mind. I am not a great fan of sport but even I know that the lanyard my job has afforded me is a great honour and privilege – a backstage pass to the most exciting event to take place in the UK for years, not forgetting the Oyster card giving you unlimited travel on the London Underground from June through to September.

This, in the end, is what most of my friends are envious of – not the incredible access to the greatest sporting show on earth, but the ability to ride around on the tube like the Queen. 'You jammy cow,' say my new flatmates when I come home with my new Oyster card in Olympic colours. 'I bet you get to use the special Olympics bus lanes as well.' It's like I've been given a private jet and a phalanx of servants, too.

Every morning, I leave the flat I now share with Harry to write 'colour' pieces about the events taking place that day. One moment I'm off to cover kayaking, the next I am bothering Bradley Wiggins for quotes about how it feels to win another gold. I hardly need to tell you that these are not sporting reports, but jolly dispatches that give a sassy sideways glance at things. As a woman who does features, I am seemingly incapable of giving something a straightforward glance, or a downwards one either.

But it's a wonderful honour, getting to cover the Olympics. It's a wonderful honour, and do you know how I deal with it? Crying, that's how. As I stand in the velodrome ten metres away from Sir Chris Hoy as he wins his sixth gold medal, I am crying. As I sit on Centre Court at Wimbledon watching Andy Murray beat Roger Federer, I am crying. As Super Saturday unravels in front of my eyes at the Olympic Stadium, Jessica Ennis taking the gold, then Greg Rutherford, then Mo Farah, I am crying. At the closing ceremony, as Take That belt out 'Rule the World' and Seb Coe makes a speech about the greatness of the preceeding two weeks, I am crying. And although I try to put it down to the pure emotion of the Olympics, the majesty and splendour and collective joy, something is nagging at me, telling me that it might be more than just that. On the train back from Stratford that night, I am still crying. 'I think that something might be wrong with you,' says a colleague with an ever-so-slightly concerned look on his face. The words echo in my head: I think he might be right.

Life seems pretty perfect, even if I am not. I have a lovely boyfriend, a great job, and yet in the days after the Olympics, I am in a funk. I tell myself it is because I've worked twenty-eight days straight without any time off. I tell myself that it is because I'm tired and on a sort of emotional comedown from the excitement of everything. I tell myself that this, too, will pass.

It's not a depression, I don't think. I'd recognise it if it was. It's a purely physical slump. In the mornings I can barely move my head off the pillow and by the afternoon I am already dreaming of sleep. When I go past restaurants, the smell makes me feel sick and the thought of alcohol has me turning my nose up in despair. We have a party to go to at the end of the week but I am not sure if I have the energy, which is *really* not like me. I've been to parties with chest infections. I've been to parties on two hours' sleep. 'Pull yourself together,' I tell myself, but by 9 p.m. I am completely slaughtered and by 10 p.m. I am back at the flat vomiting onto the carpet.

Harry and I have an argument. He tells me this has to stop, this habit of getting so drunk he has to carry me home.

'My drink must have been spiked,' I wail in my defence.

'Bryony, we were at a party with friends. Who would want to spike your drink?'

'Mr Perfect,' I start to taunt. 'That's you. I'm Harry, I don't get pissed, I don't smoke, I don't do drugs, I just sit and judge anyone who does. God, I wish that sometimes you'd just FUCK UP like everyone else.'

He doesn't rise to it. I throw up again.

The next day I try to have a cup of coffee and a cigarette – my normal hangover cure – but they only make me feel worse. At work I sit quietly at my desk

231

with a thumping headache, and by the middle of the afternoon it starts to dawn on me what could be wrong. I am late. Or more to the point, my period is. But that can't be it. I mean, I've grown up reading the *Daily Mail* and I know better than anyone that women are not allowed to have a career and a family, because in the unlikely event that this does happen, they usually end up with cancer, or heart disease. No, I can't be pregnant. This must be an anomaly caused by the madness of the Olympics. I've probably picked up a virus, or made myself ill from stress.

But something inside me makes me go home via Boots, where I buy the cheapest pregnancy test known to mankind and hide it at the bottom of my handbag. Something makes me show it to Harry once I get home, who nods silently as I disappear into the loo and remove the test from its wrapper. 'Results within three minutes!' the packet says cheerfully. I pee onto the stick. It takes just thirty seconds. One line, two lines, and the course of our whole lives changes forever.

10

I think I might be pregnant

If I were a rational person, a sane one, a human of reasonable mind, I would describe the scene in front of me as heaven on earth. 'This is heaven,' I would say, flourishing an arm towards a palm tree, and not at all minding the cliché because . . . well, because there are palm trees, people. 'This is paradise,' I would elaborate, beckoning over a waiter to clean my sunglasses and spritz me in mineral water, as if I were an exquisite rose, which of course I am – remember, we are in a parallel universe, where I do not have mental illness or gas or thighs like tree trunks or loads of really weird skin tags under my armpits that people stare at when I stretch into a yawn while wearing a strappy top. I would point to the white sand and the turquoise waters and the baby turtles within the turquoise waters that you can snorkle out to see or alternatively spend 30 Eastern Caribbean dollars admiring from a glass-bottomed boat. And I would make a joke about a passage in Luke 23:43, because in this other universe I am knowledgeable like that, and have actually read the Bible, as well as *War and Peace*, and *A Brief History of Time*, too. I will make a joke about this passage in which it was written: 'and Jesus said unto him, verily I say unto thee, today shalt thou be with me in paradise where there are glass-bottomed boats and topless dreadlocked men trying to sell you aloe vera for your sunburn – for paradise is verily close to the sun and nothing but factor 50 will cut it.'

I would take a picture of a clever book – probably something by Donna Tartt, or maybe Margaret Atwood – resting on my legs in front of a sunset, and I would post it on Instagram with a caption that said something like: #heaven #paradise #nofilterneededinheavenobv #lookhowcleveriamreadingthisbook.

But as you know by now, I am not a rational person, or a sane one, and at this very moment I am not of reasonable mind. And I can't describe the scene in front of me as heaven, because heaven is a Bad OCD Word. It is a Bad Word because, despite all its connotations of blissful happiness, it is fundamentally a place you go to when you die. And death, I am sure most of you will agree, is a bad thing. It is something to be avoided at all costs, especially if, like me, you are thirty-two years old and six months pregnant and engaged to be married to a lovely chap after a decade or so of chaotic, single misery, where your biggest commitment was to a Marlboro Light and your longest serving flatmates were a family of silverfish who lodged in the dank, mouldy bathroom.

It would be foolish, I think, to die at this point; a total and utter screw-up. After spending so long getting things so very, very wrong, I cannot quite believe that I might have somehow done something right. Some people would revel in this good fortune, but me? I'm just looking for the catch. I'm expecting a but. I'm waiting for the caveat. Fucking things up at the last moment is one of my greatest fears. It would be just like me to snatch defeat from the jaws of victory. Consequently, I live in a permanent state of anxiety. I am a meerkat constantly poised to flee from danger. So even here, on our 'babymoon' to Barbados (I know, I make myself sick even if you take away the pregnancy-induced nausea), I am primed for everything to go terribly, terribly wrong. I refuse to describe the place as heavenly lest this turns out to tempt fate. I could go for a swim and get sucked down by an invisible rip tide, or accidentally eat the fruit of the poisonous manchineel tree over there. (A sign on it warns of the dangers, but what if I were to doze off on my sun lounger and then sleep walk over and pick one up and eat it while nobody was looking? Hmmm? Did you even consider that?) I could go for a stroll on the beach and get a splinter from a felled coconut shell and the splinter could go septic and give me septicaemia and that would be it. And you may say 'don't be so ridiculous, as if that ever happens', but believe me, it does. I've read about it on Google, so it must be true.

All over, because of a stupid little splinter.

I lie on my sun lounger and imagine the newspaper reports, if indeed I warrant anything more than a paragraph. 'It's such a waste,' someone would say. 'She went through drugs and alcohol abuse and was treated badly by many different men, but she'd finally found happiness with her boyfriend. He had proposed weeks earlier, on Christmas Day, in the flat they had bought together, and they were excitedly making plans for parenthood. This trip to Barbados was supposed to be a treat. It's so sad.'

I look over at my fiancé. He is snoring gently under a book about macroeconomics, which would in itself be a heavenly sentence to write were I not plagued by the fear that describing it as heavenly means he is going to end up dead, suffocating under the book's pages. (Has anyone ever died from a paper cut across the throat? I must look that up when I have signal again.)

'Harry,' I whisper, leaning over to tap him on the shoulder. His snores momentarily get louder in response, before returning to soft, gentle grunts. 'HARRY!' I say, taking the book about macroeconomics and swatting his lounger with it.

'What?' he says. He sits upright and turns to me as if he hasn't been asleep at all.

'I'm not feeling great,' I say.

'Do you need some water?'

'No, it's not water I need. I . . .' He stares at me expectantly. 'I've just been imagining all the ways I could die on this holiday.'

'Right,' says Harry, reaching over to put his hands on my knees. 'That sounds like a lovely way to pass the time, but have you thought about reading your book, perhaps? Or maybe we could go for a walk, or a swim?'

'Harry, you have to listen to me.'

'I'm listening, Bryony. I want to be able to help you.'

'Do you think that thinking about all the ways I could die on this holiday means I might actually die on this holiday? I mean, do you think I'm going to die? Do you think it's a sign?'

'I think it's just thoughts.' He shakes his head. 'If everything that popped into our minds actually came true, the world would be chaos.'

'All my thoughts feel like ominous prophecies. They all feel like warnings.' I look up at the sky, which is clear blue, and yet despite this it feels like it is going to fall in. It feels like the whole beach is going to go up in flames leaving ashes and darkness in its place.

'Do you know, when we got off the plane the other day, I actually felt like I'd survived the plane journey? Like I'd been through some sort of ordeal and not sat there watching movies and eating crisps.'

'What do you mean, you felt like we'd survived the plane journey?' He's moved closer to me now, perhaps so nobody can hear.

'I mean, it didn't crash.'

'Yes, but that's not the same as surviving a plane journey. That's just going on a plane journey.'

'Harry, I think you should know now that you're having a child with a woman who feels she's survived every flight, rather than gone on it.'

'That's good to know. Thanks.'

'Anyway, so we survived the flight, but I just feel all of this anxiety all the time that something is going to go wrong. I mean here we are on this lovely holiday together, freshly engaged and about to become parents and with a beautiful flat in London that has a garden – I mean, we have a flat with a *garden*, even if it's really just a small patch of gravel and weeds – and yet, I can't stop worrying. I mean, what if we left the iron on and the flat has burnt down? Why didn't I bring the iron with us? It's as if my brain is trying to fill the space recently vacated by work worries with other worries. But that's not the point of a holiday, is it? You're supposed just to leave the space empty. Deliciously, vapidly empty, like a Barbie doll. But my brain won't allow it. It wants to play worry whack-a-mole. Every time I try to reassure myself that all's well, it says, "No can do! I need some sort of worry to function properly!" So I worry about the meat not being cooked properly or accidentally swigging a glass of vodka thinking it's water. I worry that the heat is going to upset the baby and I worry that I haven't felt the baby kick for at least fifteen minutes. I worry that my boss is going to forget me when I go on maternity leave and then I worry that by thinking about maternity leave I'm getting ahead of myself because what if something goes wrong between now and then? That happens all the time, doesn't it? You can never relax, never, ever.'

'But that's normal,' says Harry, coming to sit next to me on my lounger, putting his arms around me. 'You're pregnant. You're bound to be more worried than normal.'

'But I'm *always* worried, Harry. I worry when I don't have anything to worry about because the moment you take your foot off the gas then something is bound to go wrong. It just is. And I know that the moment I stop worrying and start relaxing, this whole precious thing we've built together is going to fall apart. Don't you see that if I'm worried about something, at least I have the power to try to stop it from happening?' I am crying now – the first person ever to cry while on a tropical holiday on a beach in Barbados. I must look ridiculous, but I am too upset to care. 'I worry that you might leave me, or that I might do something to hurt you, or that . . .' I am sobbing gutturally now, and Harry has clutched me to his chest, warm and comforting and smelling of him. If I could just stay here forever. If he could just hold me here until all of the stuff in my head goes away.

'It's OK, darling, it's OK. It's just your OCD.'

'But what if it's not, what if it's not? What if . . .' I note that a couple are standing under the dangerous manchineel tree staring at me, but the tears have at least scared off the hawkers and their wares. I am heaving now, tears and snot mixing together on poor Harry's chest, and that isn't even the worst of it. The worst of it is yet to come. 'I worry that . . .'

SOB.

'I worry that, what if this baby isn't yours?'

And then I collapse into his lap, and he gathers me up and takes me back to our room, where we can at least do this in some sort of privacy.

It's quite common, apparently, in pregnant women with OCD, for them to become anxious about the provenance of the child in their womb, because OCD will always latch on to the most important thing in your life at the time, and then try to threaten its existence in your life. The perinatal therapist I am seeing at the time, the one I am actually ordered to see by my GP, who is concerned about the deep depression that pregnancy hormones seem to have created inside me, tells me to imagine OCD as a person, as this will help me externalise the condition.

'I've decide to imagine OCD as Jareth the Goblin King,' I tell Harry after one of my sessions.

'Jareth the who?'

'You know! David Bowie in *Labyrinth* – big blond spiky hair, lots of make-up, disturbing silver leggings that expose a little too much. He's evil, but ever so slightly enticing, so I've decided to make him my OCD person.'

So here we are, on our babymoon in Barbados, and I have just announced to Harry that Jareth the Goblin King is trying to convince me that the baby I am having isn't his (isn't Harry's, I should point out – I mean, clearly it isn't the child of Jareth the Goblin King.)

And what's funny is that when I look back at the pictures from that holiday, there is little to suggest that it was anything other than . . . well, heavenly. There we are on the plane out – business class, if you please, after a kindly upgrade – cuddling on a flat bed, Harry grinning widely with a glass of champagne in hand. There we are having a beautiful dinner on the beach, or lying in a hammock, or, finally worn down by the hawkers, on a bloody glass-bottomed boat, thumbs held aloft to the camera.

We both remember it as a lovely holiday, and it was,

it really was, in much the same way as one remembers childbirth incredibly fondly despite screaming blue murder at the time. Harry tells me now that he can't even remember that moment on the beach when I suggested I may have slept with a stranger while out of it on a night out, only to have blanked it because of the trauma or the alcohol. He tells me he has no real memory of me going over and over this possibility, like a broken record, or the texts I sent to male friends I had seen around the time I must have conceived, asking if I had done anything I shouldn't have with them – 'Hey xx, I know I am being completely mental here, but we didn't ever, you know, back on that night in July when we all went out and got smashed?'

Can you imagine being so mad that you would actually send that to someone? And the reply, which I would check my phone every ten seconds for, would eventually come, inevitably saying something like: 'Are you completely mad? No, of course we didn't! xx' And I would feel a flood of relief for one tiny second before my brain noted this flood of relief and went, 'Hey! I'm getting the sense that you might actually be relaxing, and I'm going to ask you, for your own good, to STOP THAT RIGHT NOW. So you may not have slept with John on that night out, but what about Richard? Or what about the cab driver who took you back that evening? There's no way of contacting him, so you're going to have to latch on to that worry until all your worst fears are confirmed and you give birth to a Mexican baby, or a Chinese one, or whatever the nationality of the cab driver was, because it was so long ago you can't actually remember, and then Harry will leave you in disgust and this perfect, wonderful utopia you have created will collapse and nobody will ever speak to you ever again, not even your own mother, because everyone loves Harry and how could you have hurt him like this?'

Harry says he doesn't remember me positing the cab driver theory on him, and that he doesn't remember telling me that even if I gave birth to this imaginary cab driver's baby, he would still stay with me. He says he doesn't remember any of this because he knew it was just Jareth the Goblin King playing up, and he knew I needed support, not expressions of horror, but I think he is just being kind to me, and I wish I could have been kinder to him at the time. What I will say is this: mental illness can make you staggeringly selfish. Sometimes, the noise inside your head becomes so utterly intolerable that you don't for a minute stop to think of how it might make anyone else feel. And I'm really, truly sorry for that. To my family and my friends and my husband-to-be, who put up with these aspects of my personality because 'hey, it's just how Bryony is!', I am so so so so sorry.

If I didn't know I was pregnant, I would honestly think I was dying. I would think I had a terrible terminal illness and only months left to live. An archer, funnier person – Chloe, perhaps – would say that this was exactly what was happening to me, but I'm too strung out to make jokes, too zapped of energy and filled with nausea to come up with any witty one-liners. Instead, I lie very still in bed, incapable of turning my head from left to right without feeling like I'm on a waltzer fairground ride, wondering how any woman managed to get through this before the widespread introduction of proper doctors and Clearblue pregnancy tests. Did they say their farewells, take themselves off to a hut in the woods and wallow there for months, believing their swelling abdomens to be some terrible, pustular abomination, a form of disease-related fluid retention? Did they weep and wail alone as they went through what they presumed to be the end, the splitting in two of their vaginas, only to find that, actually, they weren't on their way out at all, but having a baby? Is this what it takes to create life – the slow but sure depletion of your own?

I know, I know. Trust me to turn something wonderful into something terrible. Trust me to make a mountain out of a molehill. Some people get pregnant, celebrate it, deal with the inevitable sickness and get on with their lives. They don't whinge about it to everyone they see and act like they are the first person in the history of the world ever to have a baby. But me? I behave as if I am Eve. I behave as if I am the Virgin bloody Mary. Sure, women have been pregnant before, but none of them have been pregnant like this.

Partly, my intolerable behaviour is because I am in shock. Harry is, too. When you find out you are pregnant for the first time, you imagine that your beloved's reaction will be to embrace you while you both jump for joy, but I just sit on the toilet sobbing in silence while Harry, a non-smoker, takes my packet of Marlboro Lights and goes straight to the garden where he lights one after another, coughing and spluttering while simultaneously managing to maintain a stupefied look on his face. (Wouldn't you look like this, too, once you'd realised your genes had been spliced with those of an actual mentalist?) I can't work out if this is some sort of act of kindness to remove all temptation from my path or if he is just stressed. I prefer to think it is the former, because that's it, cigarettes gone, and I won't be puffing on one of them for a very long time indeed . . . if indeed I ever smoke or drink or have fun again.

'I had a plan,' he says, when he comes back into the living room.

'A what?' I say, gagging at the stench of fag smoke.

'I had a plan. I thought we could be together for a couple of years, buy a flat, then in, say, 2015, I'd propose.'

'In 2015?' I almost choke on the words. 'You thought you'd propose in THREE YEARS' TIME?'

'It seemed like a reasonable period of time to me,' he says, sensibly.

'You think I would have waited around for THREE YEARS?' I say, indignant. Of course I would have done. I wasn't exactly falling over myself for bright, kind, handsome left-handers who can do Donald Duck impressions, was I? But right now, he doesn't need to know that. Right now, he can feel as crap as I do. It seems only fair.

'Well, I'm sorry I've ruined your highly romantic plan. I'm sorry I've messed with your strategy. In future, should I ring your secretary and schedule it in?'

'I don't have a secretary,' he says.

I burst into tears again. Luckily, our flatmates are out. Harry crosses the room and puts his arms around me.

'Life is what happens when you're busy making plans,' he whispers in my ear. 'I think that's what they say. I'm sorry if I seem insensitive. I'm just . . .' He puts his hands on my shoulders and looks me straight in the eye, a nervous smile breaking out over his face, like a wintery sunrise. 'I'm just going to be a father.'

I go to the doctor, because I think that is what you're supposed to do in these situations. He gives me a rough due date – some time in mid-April 2013 – a prescription for iron tablets and a recommendation that I also take folic acid, and the advice not to do any heavy lifting or gardening. 'That shouldn't be too hard to follow,' I say, trying to keep a straight face. Honestly, has he mistaken me for some sort of fully functioning human? I go to Waterstones and buy some books, which are so large that carrying them probably counts as heavy lifting – *Your Pregnancy, Day by Day, Your Pregnancy Bible, What to Expect When You're Expecting,* and so on and so on. My God! These books. They should come with a warning on them. I can't take a hot bath because, apparently, hot baths can cause spina bifida in babies. I must not eat runny eggs, certain types of cheeses, sea food, cured meats – basically, all the things I have been living off since getting together with Harry. As an obsessive compulsive who is already pretty risk-averse, pregnancy is a veritable theme park of worries. It's fucking Disney World, without any of the nice, calm rides.

Even so, I stop taking my antidepressants because surely that's the right thing to do for the baby? If I'm not allowed to take paracetamol, I don't need a doctor to tell me that bucket loads of antidepressants are bad. Some of them might change the foetus's brain chemistry, make it as screwed up as I am, and that's not something I would wish on anyone. So goodbye fags, goodbye antidepressants . . . in fact, goodbye everything my body has relied on for most of its adult life. I can't tell if my nausea is pregnancy or withdrawal, if the brain zaps are the lack of drugs or the brand new bunch of cells in my womb. My body is a confused mess, going cold turkey from various ingrained habits

247

while simultaneously trying to create a baby. It's a wonder I didn't die, really, when you think about it.

You are led to believe that one of the good things about getting pregnant is that you won't have to deal with periods for nine months, but being pregnant feels like you're about to get your period, only constantly. Plus, if the books are to be believed, once you've given birth, you bleed for a month and have to wear nappies like your newborn. It's as if God is punishing you for having the gall to have ovaries, while your other half gets to go and get pissed at the pub.

The nausea sits with me constantly, like a stalker I cannot shake off, and when I do manage to get a restraining order, I just worry that the reason it is not there is because I am no longer pregnant. I piss on five more sticks just to be sure that I am. The woman in Boots cannot look at me as she scans every test the store has to offer, because clearly I am a lunatic stockpiling for the pregnancy apocalypse. Whatever. I *am* deranged. You would be, too, if you felt you were permanently being punched in the tits, which have, incidentally, gone a strange, deep purple, like children's party balloons, only not quite as much fun. And my vagina feels violent. My vagina has never felt violent. Do you know what it feels like to have a violent vagina? It feels angry and cross and a little bit stabby. And then sometimes it feels just like the sensation heart-attack patients say they had in their chest – like an elephant is sitting on it.

I go back to the doctor, who thankfully is female this time.

'It feels like there's an elephant sitting on my vagina,' I say.

'That's normal,' she replies. 'And I hate to tell you that it's only going to get worse.'

It's only going to get worse because I'm not even six weeks pregnant. I've been with child for all of about ten minutes, yet the way I'm going on about it, you'd think I was ready to give birth. Nope. Seven and a bit more months of this, I'm afraid. Seven and a bit more months. Sorry, Harry. Sorry, everyone.

You're not supposed to tell anyone that you're pregnant before twelve weeks, but then you're not supposed to tell anyone that you're having an affair, are you? And getting pregnant with a man you love seems far less shameful than that. Plus, if something did go wrong, why are women expected to carry it around like some humiliating secret? How is anyone meant to get through the misery of miscarriage if they are made to feel like pariahs when they have one? Shhh, keep it to yourself, as if you have gonorrhea or leprosy or scabies and your body didn't just make a mistake.

So I decide to tell my family and a couple of friends and my boss. I practise what I am going to say to them in the mirror. 'So, there's something I've got to tell you,' I trill, bright and breezy, so they don't think I'm about to tell them I have, say, a drug addiction, or huge gambling debts, or cancer. 'There's something I've got to tell you. I'm going to be a MOTHER. A M-O-T-H-E-R. Harry and I are going to have a BABY. A B-A-B-Y.'

Chloe is not surprised. She's not anything, really. 'Poor Harry,' she says, in her dry, Chloe way. 'That poor baby.' My mum bursts into tears, my father asks who the father is, my sister squeals, 'YOU'RE SAVED!' and my brother says, 'That's cool, but also kind of gross.' At work, people just want to tell me about postpartum constipation.

It's so like me to make the decision to tell a few people, only to feel bad about making the decision to tell a few people. I start to think I am tempting fate and will be punished for not being a good pregnant woman and keeping my 'condition' to myself. Billions of other women manage it, Bryony, so why can't you? It's as if the words that come out of my mouth might have some bearing on the health of the foetus inside me, just as I've always thought the words that come out of my mouth might have some bearing on the health of the people around me. I don't deserve to be pregnant, I reason. I have no right to be pregnant, after everything I have done. Why do I get this happy outcome when so many others who have never smoked nor drunk excessively, who have never misbehaved, cannot manage to conceive?

When I am six and a half weeks pregnant, I have a bad day at work. A really bad day at work. The worst since I had to write up an interview with Mickey Rooney on a coke comedown and absolutely no sleep. It's a Friday and I have a big deadline for the next-day's paper, but I keep on making mistakes that aren't like me. I can't manage to get the words out, let alone put them on my computer screen. It's only a piece about the Duchess of Cambridge and how her tour of south-east Asia has been disrupted by the publication of some long-ago-taken topless sunbathing pictures – all my favourite subjects, basically – but I am incapacitated by incompetence. I'm mangling sentences, creating errors, repeating them all over the place. At 4 p.m., my boss pulls me aside and tells me to go home. 'You look exhausted,' she says. 'I've asked the royal correspondent to finish this off and he says it won't be a problem.'

I've never before given up halfway through a piece. Normally, having to say no to something sends me into a downward spiral of paranoia about whether or not I am about to be sacked, but on this particular day I feel I have no choice. I don't even care. I switch off my computer, utter some meagre thank yous and good-byes, and leave the office via the loos, because already my bladder is a cliché, already it doesn't seem able to go twenty minutes without calling to be emptied. I pull down my jeans, sit down on the toilet, and think for a moment about falling asleep there, but the red colour of my knickers stuns me into alertness. Reader, since getting together with Harry and putting on weight, I do not own any red knickers, let alone any sexy ones. I long ago realised that these were pointless indulgences, given that most men just want to take them off. And the ones I put on this morning were pale blue. Now they are not. Now they are stained dark with blood.

I stand up, turn nervously to look in the toilet bowl. More blood. I wipe. More blood. My knees go weak and I hold on to the side of the cubicle to steady myself. I note that there is blood on the floor, too. There is a sense of dawning horror but also a strange acceptance of what seems to be happening, because of course I wouldn't hold on to this pregnancy. Of course this wasn't meant to be.

I stuff some tissue paper in my knickers, pull up my trousers, leave the cubicle, wash my hands, think of Harry, just across the office, completely unaware of the events unfolding right now in my underwear. I rummage for my phone in my handbag, find a quiet corner and call him. 'I'm, I'm, I'm bleeding,' I barely whisper down the line, and within three minutes he is with me, within four he is bundling us into a cab and within twenty we are at the nearest A&E.

The driver drops us off at Chelsea and Westminster hospital and as we get out I note Hugh Grant crossing over the road. 'Hugh Grant,' I say to Harry, once the actor is out of earshot. 'Hugh Grant.' Harry looks at Hugh Grant, nods, and then directs me towards the doors of the building. 'At least you're still able to celeb spot,' he says. 'That must be a good sign.'

Inside, a receptionist asks what is wrong. 'I think I'm having a miscarriage,' I manage to tell her, and she hands me a form over the counter, as if this is just an everyday occurrence, which when I think about it, it almost certainly is. We sit down in a waiting area, next to a man with his foot packed with frozen peas. I attempt to make light conversation in an effort to distract myself from what is going on. 'Think I broke it playing football,' he explains, but he doesn't ask what is wrong with me because it is clear that whatever it is, it isn't the kind of thing you talk about in public.

After an hour that feels like six but is actually only about five minutes in Accident and Emergency time, I am called through to a private room with its own door. It's early evening but already I can hear the Friday night drunks who are a feature of hospital casualty departments, and I am thankful for that door. I lie down on the cold, hard bed. Harry sits on a plastic chair and stares at the ceiling as if it might provide us with some answers. Someone tells us that a doctor will be with us shortly, and I actually go to my handbag to pull out the book I am reading, *World War Z*, a zombie novel that could not be more inappropriate if it tried.

Eventually, a young, female doctor arrives, and she examines me as kindly as one can examine a cervix, before taking some blood, giving me some sanitary pads and putting me on a drip. Then she disappears, and Harry says, 'It's going to be OK,' again and again, but an hour later she is back, bearing a sad face and bad news.

'So we're going to send you home, Bryony,' she says. 'We can't say for sure, but we think you might be having a miscarriage. I want you to go home and rest. I've got you the first appointment I can at the early pregnancy unit. They'll be able to tell you more on Monday morning.'

Monday morning, I think, and then we catch a cab so that we can maybe have a miscarriage in the comfort of our own home.

They call it maternal instinct, don't they? But I had no idea it would kick in this soon. We get home, order Chinese – who orders Chinese when they've just been told they might be miscarrying? – and I fall asleep with several sanitary pads stuffed in my knickers. In the morning I wake up and there is no blood on them. Everything seems to have stopped. 'Deep down, I feel like everything is going to be OK,' I say for the first time in my life, although, of course, I can't know for sure, just as I can't say for sure that chanting 'I'd rather I died than my family' has been the reason everyone has – touch wood, touch wood a thousand times – stayed alive. Of course, my instinct could prove to be nothing more than desperation, but sometimes, you'll cling to anything, won't you? You'll hold on to the slimmest of hopes just to get through.

The early pregnancy unit is – cruelly – located right next to the maternity ward. It is the kind of place you should dread going to, and yet, strangely, I cannot wait to be there, to get everything out of the way. Across the room, another couple look pale, sad. I wonder if they, too, are overwhelmed with love for something that just six weeks ago they didn't even know they wanted. A voice calls my name and we make our way into a small room containing another cold, hard bed, a computer, and a woman brandishing something that I would describe as looking like a dildo if I was in a better mood.

She tells me to hop on to the bed and pull down my knickers, and then she explains that she is going to scan me internally to see if she can find a heartbeat. It shouldn't be too uncomfortable, she says. I do as I am told and close my eyes as Harry squeezes my hand and this stranger roots around inside me, and then she says, 'Ahah!' and I open my eyes and on the screen I see a bean-shaped creature and a flashing light, which the woman tells me is a heartbeat.

'Congratulations,' she says.

A heartbeat! We are actually having a baby, people!

But as you know by now, I have an uncanny ability to replace one ordeal with another.

At about ten weeks, just before your twelve-week scan, pregnant women have what is known as a 'booking-in appointment'. This involves a midwife working out what kind of birth you want to have – as if you really have any choice in the matter – and taking urine and blood 'to test for various things', as she says to me before sticking a needle in my arm.

'What things?' I ask, my interest piqued.

'Oh you know. Hepatitis. Syphillis. HIV.'

I leave the doctor's surgery in a state of blind panic. I am twelve years old again, but the difference here is that there is a genuine, legitimate possibility that I could be HIV positive. A decade or so of sex while either high on drugs or pissed as a newt or both must put me in the high-risk category, surely? I always tried to be safe but there are gaps in my memory and besides, you never can be 100 per cent certain, can you? What about the cab journeys home I don't remember, and the lost hours in nightclubs and bars? Then there are the things you do recall, but would rather forget.

Harry and I are going to see Michael McIntyre that night on some sort of work jolly, but I feel unable to laugh at his jokes about dishwashers and man drawers and all the other normal things that my head – or Jareth the Goblin King, to be precise – will not let me enjoy. He won't let me enjoy them because how could I, when there is every possibility I have denied such simple day-to-day pleasures to my boyfriend and my unborn child, whom I have quite possibly infected with HIV? Of course, it's important to point out here that if I was thinking straight, I would know that there is absolutely no reason to feel ashamed about such an outcome because HIV is now as manageable as asthma, and more manageable than diabetes, and nobody deserves a disease no matter what they do. But I am not thinking straight, not at all. I'm looking for reasons to punish myself. I'm trying to find the thing that is inevitably going to go wrong.

I don't spend the next day looking at babygros or booties or potential buggies. I spend it Googling the rates of male-to-female HIV transmission, and reacquainting myself with the symptoms of the illness. I call up the hotline of the Terence Higgins Trust, and list all the ways I think I could have been infected to a patient man who is infected. He is kind, considerate, thoughtful, even when I call him back the next day, and the one after that. (Reader, I gave the charity a handsome donation in an attempt to assuage my conscience.) The orange book the midwife gave me shortly after taking my blood, the one I am to carry to every antenatal appointment, contains a number to call if you have any concerns. I reason that I do, and ask the woman on the other end of the phone if my blood-test results are in yet. 'Not for another week or so, love,' she says. 'Now go and put your feet up.'

But I can't. I can't because what if I am killing my unborn child and the father of my unborn child without them even knowing it? Every day I call the hospital line, and every day the same woman answers, a weary sound in her voice. 'Pregnancy does funny things to a woman,' she says one day, in an attempt at comforting me, and I want to reply, 'In this case, not just pregnancy. In this case, EVERYTHING!' When she is eventually able to tell me that all my results have come back negative, she sounds as relieved as I am.

Even then my brain is incapable of relaxing and accepting that, in all probability, everything will be OK. It spits at comforting probabilities and throws back terrifying ones. It answers 'that's unlikely' with endless bloody 'what ifs?' One reassurance only leaves space for a new, more terrifying anxiety. The egg I had from the canteen might not have been cooked properly and it might give me salmonella. My friend's cat might have given me listeria. The baby might not be Harry's. I obsess over conception dates. I scrutinise my phone bill to make sure there aren't any strange numbers that could belong to men I have blanked from my memory banks. And the logical part of my mind tells me that this is OCD, this is Jareth, feeding on my greatest fears and breeding more. But the OCD tells me it is real.

And the anger. The anger is unlike anything I have

ever experienced before. This is a different kind of madness, a dangerous kind. With the OCD at least a part of me tries to be rational, but now I have the ability to explode in complete, pure rage, seemingly for no reason at all. I throw phones at windows and smash them, the phones and the windows. I ring Harry eighty-seven times when he is twenty minutes late home. Some people thank the iPhone for giving them a camera in their pocket, or a ready connection to social media, but for me the starkest thing is how, in little brackets after my boyfriend's name, it has the ability to show me what a nutter I am.

One day a flatmate mentions that he has seen a mouse in the living room, and I quietly go to our room where I pack a suitcase and leave home. I walk for three miles before Harry finds me, shaking and crying on a park bench on a dark, Saturday night, but I refuse to go back. I refuse to be poisoned by the mouse. 'We have to go to a hotel!' I scream, scaring dog walkers and my boyfriend, and so we hand over £169 to spend a night in a four-star establishment I deem clean enough.

We are trying to club together what little capital we have to buy a place of our own, because babies can't be brought up in flatshares, can they? Every weekend and most weekday evenings we go to look at places but none seem suitable. I swear that all of them contain hidden dangers that will bring an end to what little happiness we have left. 'Let me tell you now,' I state, while waiting outside a house for an estate agent to arrive, 'I WILL NEVER LIVE IN THIS FLAT.' There's no reason for my refusal other than irrational anger, and a week later we put an offer in on the flat we still live in to this day.

Harry looks beaten. He looks like a man under attack. He's having to stroke my back every night for three hours to help me get to sleep. He's having to soothe the unsoothable. He's having to ease the transition from Bryony Gordon: Party Girl to Bryony Gordon: Mother, the one that involves endless nightmares that I have taken cocaine and lost the baby. Every time I manage to fall asleep, they are there. But what kind of living nightmare is he going through? How is this fair to him? We can't continue like this. *I* can't continue like this, because if I do, we will both be emotionally destroyed by the time the baby arrives. And I have to start thinking about my unborn child, as well as my other half. I have to, because it isn't fair to bring another human into this misery. It isn't fair to potentially pass my mental-health issues on to a complete innocent. After all, this baby won't have asked to be born. 'I think you need to go back on antidepressants,' Harry says to me, when I am five months pregnant and have shouted at him for cooking a spaghetti bolognese the wrong way. 'I think you need to for the sake of your mental health, for the sake of our relationship, and for the sake of our child.' And I know he is right. I know that, despite the tiny risks of autism and birth defects that can come with taking some types of antidepressant while pregnant, the risks to all of us if I don't are far greater. This isn't just about the here and now. It's about our long-term future.

First, I have to go to Miami on a work trip. Me, Jareth the Goblin King, pregnancy hormones and a ten-hour flight – the combination is just perfect, isn't it? Every time we hit turbulence, which is often, I cry and talk to my already huge bump, apologising for putting the life inside it in great peril by having the audacity to take it on a plane.

Two small children are sitting a few rows behind me, and Jareth keeps asking me if I have dragged them into the toilet and done terrible things to them. Of course I haven't, but by this point Jareth is throwing me curveballs in the form of 'what ifs' every few minutes, and I barely have the energy to catch them.

When I get to the hotel, I notice there is a spa and so, in desperation to feel just a tiny bit better, I book a pregnancy massage. Pregnancy massages are almost universally awful because all the practitioners can do is basically stroke you sympathetically as you lie on your side feeling more and more irritated by the fact that all they can do is stroke you sympathetically, because they can't put pressure on certain points in your shoulders and feet and even ears as it might be damaging to the foetus.

Anyway, for some reason I think things might be different in America, where the portion sizes and lack of gun control seem to show scant regard for health and wellbeing. 'The woman who will be doing my treatment probably has three handguns and five assault rifles to her name as well as a massage qualification,' I muse, as I wait for her to arrive. 'She's definitely going to get her knuckles right in there.'

I get a sense of the disappointment I am going to experience when she appears looking like Tinker Bell in a spa uniform. She grins at me and I am almost blinded by her dazzlingly white teeth.

'Hi, I'm Jennifer and I'm going to be your spa associate today. Please tell me if there is anything I can do for you.'

Of course, I can't tell Jennifer what she can do for me – namely, give me a massage so firm that you can hear my bones crack in South Carolina. We walk to the treatment room via a 'waterless fountain of life' (a sink) containing 'precious stones' (some cheap gems that are only marginally more convincing than the ones five-year-old girls stick on their Barbie dolls). Jennifer asks me to choose one. I do as I am told and fish around in the waterless fountain of life, scooping out a yellow gem that Jennifer reveals, with a faux gasp and a coy giggle, is a signifier of fertility and health. And although I know for sure from this moment on that the massage is doomed, the cheap gemstone still remains in my wallet alongside my coins to this day, because I am too mental and super-stitious to get rid of it.

In the end, I paid $80 for that cheap stone, plus forty minutes of seething, passive-aggressive resent-ment backed by panpipe music, which I am sure you will all agree is a great deal.

'How was your treatment?' asks the girl on reception, once I have emerged feeling more exhausted than when I arrived. I am ashamed to admit that I answer her routine question by bursting into tears.

'I'm scared I'm never going to sleep again,' I wail, and to her credit she doesn't flinch at all.

'Girlfriend,' she smiles – genuinely, which seems to me a rarity in shiny, service-industry America – 'what you need is an hour with THIS man.' She pushes a leaflet in front of me advertising a new acupuncturist who has just started working at the hotel. 'You won't ever be needing a massage again once you've spent some time with him and his magic needles.'

Was this a euphemism? I hoped not. And I don't know why I thought acupuncture would work when I think homeopathy is hocus-pocus and that massage therapists are talking shite when they say that rubbing your big toe might cause you to give birth immediately. If that were the case, there would be no need for caesarian sections or vacuums that suck the baby out of your vagina, would there? But I was desperate in Miami, and I just wanted to get through the trip and home, so I booked in to see the man and his magic needles and, boy oh boy, am I glad I did.

Acupuncture is a form of Chinese Medicine, and scientists believe it works because the needles are stuck in areas where nerves, muscles and connective tissues are located, helping the blood to flow around them. All I know is that after one session I slept like a baby, rather than like there was a baby inside me, which is a very different thing. The worries about the plane seemed if not to vanish, then to at least to be a little less important. I saw the acupuncturist once more before I flew back, and I cried just once on the journey, when the woman sitting next to me spilt a Bloody Mary all over me just as I was nodding off to sleep. 'Alcohol,' I thought, 'I miss you,' but then I get home and book some more acupuncture and an appointment with the GP, and very briefly everything seems all right in the world.

The GP is horrified when I tell her I simply stopped taking my antidepressants the moment I found out I was pregnant.

'I can understand why you would do it but it's much safer to stay on them in cases such as yours.' I bristle at the accusatory tone in her voice. I don't know what she means. I've got a bit of OCD, a tendency towards mild depression. But doesn't everyone? It's not as if I'm psychotic. It's not as if I'm losing the plot.

But I'm relieved that she thinks I should go back on the drugs, this time Sertraline, which seems safe for pregnant women, and I'm relieved when she tells me she is going to refer me to an organisation called MAPPIM, which is situated at St Thomas's Hospital, where I plan to give birth. MAPPIM stands for Maternity and Perinatal Partnerships in Mental Health, although it never occurs to me to Google it at the time. Perhaps this is just as well, because I'm not sure I would have liked what I found: 'MAPPIM is a multi-disciplinary mental-health service for pregnant and postnatal women with severe and complex mental illness, having their care at St Thomas's Hospital. Referrals are essential for women with bipolar affective disorder; schizophrenia/schizoaffective disorder; previous postpartum psychosis; severe depression.'

It stuns me to read this now. At the time I thought I was being referred for some therapy, but I now realise that I was being flagged up as a serious concern. I was essentially being put on a watch list. If I'd had any awareness of this, I probably would have gone into paroxysms of paranoia that social services were going to take away my baby. But I just wanted help. I just wanted to feel myself again, whoever that person might have been. And the people at MAPPIM were the ones who gave me that help.

Was I suffering from severe depression? Almost certainly, Harry tells me now. 'You were not in a good way,' he says, in that way people can once everything has passed. People talk a lot about postnatal depression but they never tell you about perinatal depression, the bit before you give birth when you walk around in a daze, wondering what the fuck you have done. They don't tell you about the inability to get out of bed, coupled with the crippling insomnia. They don't tell you about the feeling you have where you could scratch out your eyeballs in tiredness and desperation. They don't tell you about the horrifying realisation that you cannot look after yourself, let alone anybody else.

'What a wonderful time,' people say to you. 'Enjoy it while it lasts, because you're never sleeping again once the little blighter is born!' But if this is the fun bit, what hope do I have for afterwards? If this is the good bit, would it be better if I gave the baby up for adoption now?

I tell this to the psychiatrist I have to see every two weeks for the remainder of my pregnancy – the one who suggests Jareth the Goblin King and who, I am told, will visit me frequently after the birth, just to 'check' that everything is 'OK'. I tell him this and he nods along, because he's heard it all before. He's met so many women like me, and it gives me some sort of comfort, eventually, to know that there are many others out there, like me. It pains me that anyone else might feel this way, but it brings me a strange sort of peace, too.

Professional psychiatry brings a new sense of calm. The final trimester of my pregnancy is the happiest. We move into our flat and have my family round for Christmas. In the morning, before they arrive, Harry presents me with a stocking full of presents.

'I want you to have this while it's just the two of us.' He looks at my growing bump and smiles. 'Well, just the three of us.'

We sit on the sofa and I apologise for not getting him a stocking. 'Been a lot on my mind,' I joke. Then I delve into the carefully wrapped gifts he has bought for me – a Smythson notebook, some pyjamas from Anthropologie to keep me warm, a Tiffany bracelet, and finally, a box that has engraved on it the words 'OPEN ME'. I look at him with a flicker of recognition on my face of what is about to happen. This, this is it. The baby kicks down on my vagina in a way that has become comforting, if anything. I open the box and I look at Harry and he says, very coyly, 'I think you know what that is.'

I do. It is an engagement ring. It is his late mother's engagement ring, to be precise, a sapphire surrounded by diamonds set on a gold band, but it could be anything. It could be a plastic jelly ring or a cracker ring because what really matters is the sentimental value. Not for the first time in our relationship, I start to cry.

'Why are you crying?' he asks.

'Because even though you haven't got down on one knee or actually asked me to marry you, the fact that I am heavily pregnant and we have just bought a flat suggests to me that you are about to propose.'

'Well, seeing as you've mentioned it: will you marry me?'

As if he had to ask.

As if he had to bloody ask.

I've got a doppler now, a machine that allows you to hear your baby's heartbeat at home. That makes me feel better, more relaxed. I get more acupuncture. I go swimming three times a week. As my due date nears, I start to hibernate. I cook pasta dishes, order a buggy, watch a lot of box sets. My hair has completely grown back for the first time in fourteen years, a fact I feel the need to celebrate with a post on Facebook. 'Nobody's told you about postpartum hair loss, then?' replies some smart-arse, whom I take it upon myself to defriend, because really, who needs this shit in your life? Who wants it any more?

I go on maternity leave, get into *Gossip Girl*. I'm really fucking happy at this point, I think. Chloe visits me with cake while I watch Chace Crawford and Blake Lively gallivant around Manhattan on ever-more ridiculous plot lines.

'Good to see you're not making any attempt to grow up just because you're pregnant,' she says, nudging me. 'And can I say that, even the size of a hot-air balloon, you still look pretty damn fine?'

'You can,' I smile. 'I'm going to take a compliment, for once.'

It's nice to know we have more in common than drugs and booze. It's nice to know that we are really, truly friends.

Two weeks before my due date, Harry and I settle down for a Sunday evening of posh pizza and yet more *Gossip Girl*. He pretends not to like it, but he's gone through five seasons with me. On this particular night, my favourite character, Chuck Bass – a deviant rich kid with a thing for drugs and wild women – is getting involved in a major storyline, making some pithy comments. I feel a wave of pain through my abdomen, a trickle of liquid.

'I think it's happening,' I say to Harry, and it has.

My waters have broken.

To *Gossip Girl*.

Of course they fucking have.

11

I think I might need help

Our daughter Edie is born at 2.52 p.m. on Tuesday, 9 April 2013 to the sound of me singing the *Muppet Babies* theme tune. In my defence, I am fucked. I am completely off my tits. I've had two epidurals, several lungfuls of gas and air, and about three hours' sleep in two days. I'm naked as a Norfolk dumpling and high as a kite, so what's a bit of tuneless singing between friends? I mean, once someone has shone a floodlight on your vagina and peered into it as if the FA Cup might be taking place there . . . well, anything goes. Absolutely anything. You think I did embarrassing things in my twenties? Well, let me tell you they were as nothing when compared to some of the shit I did in room nine of St Thomas's birthing centre. I hovered over a cardboard commode while vomiting onto the father of my child. I showered everyone in my blood when I accidentally pulled a cannula out of my hand thinking it was the gas and air tube. I stood at the window staring at the Houses of Parliament with nothing but a heart-rate monitor around my swollen belly and tried to make a joke about not having been this high at this time in the morning since my thirtieth birthday.

'Maybe,' said the unfortunate midwife charged with my care that morning, 'maybe you could put, like, a bra on or something?'

You think the worst thing about labour is going to be the pain, but it's not. You can forget the pain. You can forgive the pain. The pain is necessary, because it takes you towards the thing you want most. What stays with you is the steady stripping out of your inhibitions one by one, like a particularly slow, torturous bikini wax, and just when you think you can't go any lower, you realise a stranger is cleaning away a poo you didn't even know that you had done.

After my waters break, we go to the hospital and they promptly send us home again. 'Get some rest,' they say. 'Go for a walk,' they also say. Harry takes their advice. I've never been able to take advice, and so I do neither of these things. Instead, as my womb contracts and expands within me, I work. I actually bloody work. This is all happening much earlier than I thought it would – two weeks before my due date

– and I have columns for the *Sunday Telegraph* I haven't managed to file yet, and I know I won't be able to file them in the weeks after our child is born. So I sit on a birthing ball with my laptop on my knees and tap, tap, tap away while necking codeine and turning up the electrical shocks on the TENS machine that is supposed to help with the pain of the contractions, but doesn't, not really. It's like replacing one pain with another, like going to a pharmacy to ask for some medicine to help with a headache only for them to say 'here you go' before punching you in the stomach.

Eventually, some twenty-four hours later, we return to the hospital where they surmise that I have made absolutely no progress and need to be induced. They put me on a drip and now the pain starts with gusto, until, eventually, they shine that floodlight on my vagina and tell me I am ready to push. But try as I might I know deep down that this baby isn't coming out that way, and suddenly Harry is dressed in scrubs, like my very own version of George Clooney in *ER*, except there is no time to get excited about this because I am being wheeled into theatre and there are lots of people, all of whom look much younger than I am, some of whom are telling me that my baby is stuck and needs to be removed with an emergency caesarian section. 'We're sorry,' say the young doctors.

'Why are you saying sorry?' I slur. 'If it means it's actually going to be over in another couple of minutes without me having to do anything, there's really no need to apologise. Unless you're apologising because it's a terrible, painful procedure?'

'It might feel like we're doing the washing-up in you, but otherwise it's painless.'

I try to imagine what it might feel like to have the washing-up done inside me, fail, and wonder if there is time for some more gas and air.

'But you all look so young,' I manage to get out. 'And I don't mean that as a compliment. Are you sure you know what you're doing? Are you sure you're all qualified? Oh my God! I'm going to have major surgery performed on me by the surgeon equivalent of the Muppet Babies!'

'Who are the Muppet Babies?' asks someone, who must surely be an actual child.

'They were cute cartoon baby versions of the grown-up Muppets,' says the anaesthetist, as she sprays something cold on me to check I have no feeling in my legs. 'I remember the theme tune to this day . . .'

And that is how, as I am sliced open from hip to hip, I come to be singing the *Muppet Babies* song as my child is born. And I notice, as I sing it over and over again, the feeble sound of a cry that does not belong to me, although I know I am sobbing, too, because how could I not be? And I notice that the cry starts to sound less and less feeble, and starts to sound closer and closer, as our child is removed from me and placed in Harry's arms, a girl, our girl, our forever girl, and then she is against my chest, out of me but still part of me, and I hold her close to me, breathe her in, and in that moment I know more than I ever have that everything is going to be OK.

Well, come on. Let's not get carried away here. Of course it isn't going to be OK. There are going to be tears – from the baby, but mostly from me. There are going to be moments when I don't know what I am doing, when I get soaked as I struggle to put the rain-cover on the buggy for the first time in the first and only tropical storm ever to hit south-west London. There are moments when I feel like a terrible failure, like when it becomes clear that, despite my huge boobs, I cannot feed my child from them. I try and I try and I try, but she turns away from my breasts screaming – the first person ever in the history of the world to do this – and when I attempt to pump, I am a deflated dairy cow, producing nothing but a pathetic trickle that wouldn't even feed a shrew. We move to formula, and the failure turns to guilt. Will it poison her, and if it doesn't poison her, will it stunt her growth and her intelligence and lead to her failing her A-levels? But she begins to thrive and soon that worry passes, too, giving way to some new one – colic, strange rashes, strange nappies, coughs, colds, constipation, and so on and so on, until before you know it they are adults and you're fretting about what they are getting up to on nights out. So no, dealing with a newborn baby is not always OK, but it's not half as bad as I expected it to be, not nearly as galling as everyone has made it out to be. Even the sleeplessness I can deal with because after a decade of depriving myself of sleep through alcohol and drug misuse, this is more than manageable. Getting up at 5 a.m. is far better than going to bed then.

If my state of mind during pregnancy suggested to everyone that I was going to deal with motherhood badly, now the opposite is true. Although many new mothers develop OCD, perhaps because of the ridiculous hygiene levels that suddenly come into play, my experience of the illness means that these are next to nothing. Constant hand-washing doesn't bother me; sterilising is a cinch. It's as if the responsibility and the reality of looking after a newborn has hit a switch in my brain that turns off the OCD, so my brain is saying to it, 'She's got a child to look after now, so could you just fuck off please, so she can get on with being a mother?' At this point, with fatigue and hormones and a new baby, I'm not mindful enough to acknowledge that anxiety has become so normal to me, I barely realise it is there. But I guess that's a protective mechanism. I guess it's something primal kicking in, to keep us all alive.

Charged with the enormous responsibility of caring for a newborn, I do not wither but blossom. I travel on the tube across London with her strapped to my chest; I visit friends and galleries and exhibitions. We go on umpteen social engagements together and lunch regularly. We swim, we walk, we explore parts of the city I haven't bothered to venture to in all my life living in London. In part, I am trying to prove to myself and everyone around me that I can do this, but mostly I just want to prove it to her. To Edie. I want her to have not just a normal mother, but a successful one, who does the very best for her. I don't want her to see even the slightest glimpse of the woman I was before she came along. Perhaps, unrealistically, I want this barely cognisant being to think I am perfect.

Of course, there are terrible moments, like the one just days after she is born, when I feel sad because it is not just Harry and me any more; and a week later, when she won't stop crying and we go for a walk, and when she finally falls asleep in her pram, I sit down on a park bench and watch all the other families being normal and playing and feel for sure that we will never be like that. And then when Harry tells me he is going to be half an hour late home from work, and I scream down the phone at him because when you have spent a day alone with a small, crying baby, half an hour seems like half a year. 'HOW COULD YOU DO THIS TO ME?' I wail, on more than one occasion. 'HOW COULD YOU BE SO SELFISH?' There's the time he comes home and finds Edie on a playmat screaming, and me lying beside her doing exactly the same. There's the Friday afternoon when I get lost on the way to a meeting with my antenatal group and call him just to sob for ten minutes while I get my bearings. But I think these are normal. I think these are probably forgiveable. I think you'd be more weird if you didn't go slightly mad the first time you had a child.

Three months after she is born, Harry and I get married at Chelsea register office. It's a small, family affair followed by lunch at a pub. My dress costs £90 from Monsoon, and our first dance is to Take That, 'Rule the World'. 'You arranged a wedding with a tiny baby?' is the response from everyone, and even I am impressed that we managed this ridiculous feat while juggling early parenthood. It's as if it all happens in a dream-like state. In fact, in the first year of Edie's life, and for the first time in mine, I impress everyone – the MAPPIM team, who are impressed by the fact that the OCD does not seem to be manifesting itself in any way; the people I send thank-you cards to within a week of receiving their gifts; my boss at work, who cannot believe I'm OK to go and do the odd interview; my publisher, to whom I manage to turn in an entire book on time.

I feel invincible. I feel like superwoman. And then . . .
And then the darkness comes back.

It's hard for me to write about what happens next. It's
hard because when you are well, you cannot even begin
to imagine the places that you went to in your head,
and when you are not well, you do not want to write.
You do not want to write or read or do anything. I
remember that when I was ill, the only thing I wanted
to do was be run over when I crossed the road, run
over and hospitalised with a broken bone, run over
and sedated for a week, because then I'd have a reason
just to lie there without any need to explain. Then I'd
have an excuse. But this? There feels as if there is no
way to explain this.

It is December and Edie is twenty months old when
I come careering off the tracks. I thought I had
somehow beaten my OCD, that she had been the
miraculous cure for it, the one to finally beat Jareth
the Goblin King. But I was wrong. It was only a
ceasefire in hostilities, a reprieve, the calm before the
storm, if you like. What is it that causes this derail-
ment, after so long without it? How do I manage to
cope through the terrifying newborn stage, and not
at the stage when most parents are just hitting their
stride? Is it the stress of going back to work, combined
with the weirdness of having a book out, crammed
together with weeks of Christmas parties at which I

had drunk too much and failed to look after myself? Maybe. Probably. But I thought that if I could cope with a new baby, I could cope with anything. I thought I could take on the world. So why, very suddenly, do I find that I can't even take on each new day? I am crying at my desk, convinced I have hurt my daughter while changing her nappy that morning. I am hyper-ventilating in the loos at the thought that I could have molested her while tipsy after a party. I am spending every night sitting on the floor in her room next to her cot, listening to her breathing, checking she is still alive, until Harry comes and finds me and scrapes me into bed, promising everything is going to be OK, promising and promising until eventually I am too tired to put up a fight.

All the worst things that I could do to her have suddenly set up shop in the cracks of my mind. Have I sent pictures of her to paedophiles, and am I a paedo-phile myself? (Never mind the fact I don't know any paedophiles or have any knowledge of where to find them – OCD, or Jareth the Goblin King, does not operate with logic in mind.) Have I lingered too long while cleaning her, have I hurt her while giving her a bath? Have I given her an overdose of Calpol, have I put bleach in her milk? Have I sleepwalked and gone to strangle her? Could the cord from the blind five foot away from her cot somehow strangle her? Could there be a bit of string in her bed that I haven't seen that strangles her? Could her teddy bears suffocate her? Could she just stop breathing without the aid of any of these things? Might our world end just as it is getting going?

And are the police coming? They must be, mustn't they? I can see them in my mind, breaking down the front door as we all sleep, and pulling her out of her bed as I scream and she screams and everyone screams. They are coming to arrest me and they are coming to take her away. And what would I do if that happened to me? If that happened to her? I would have to kill myself, I would have to, I would have to, I would have to, I would have to. But how? And am I actually too cowardly to do it? Even if all that was actually to happen, would I be too gutless and pathetic to do the right thing?

Once more, my mind whirs not with possibility, but catastrophe. This could happen, that could happen, what if it already had happened? I am too scared to hold her close in case I hurt her, too paralysed with fear to change her nappy. When I go to pick her up from nursery, I am sure the keyworkers are looking at me in a funny way. I am sure they are poised to call social services. Of all of the attacks I have had in my life, this is the worst, because it is trying to take away from me this thing I have earned, this human I have loved and grown and nurtured and cared for. It is trying to stop me from doing the things that come most naturally to me. It is placing evil and shame where there is none, it is convincing me I am a bad mother when I am not. I am not. I am not. I. AM. NOT. But the more I tell myself this, the more I chant it and whisper it, the more OCD tries to convince me otherwise. It finds any cracks it can, any shreds of doubt, and sets up home in them, where it breeds, like fungus. Like bacteria. Like mould.

In desperation, I start to seek reassurance from Harry. 'Do you think I could have molested her?' I ask him. 'Do you think I could have done something absolutely terrible? Do you think I will lose her?'

There is a look of pure physical pain on his face, as I place in his mind the startling, terrible possibility that his wife could have hurt his own child. Her own child. And in the most appalling way. I see the pain, I see the hurt, I see the horror. But OCD has shut down any capacity I might have to behave in a selfless, caring way and not ask him things like this. It has stripped out the kindness my husband so clearly deserves. It is not just destroying me. It is destroying him, too.

Slowly but surely, OCD has taken over my head entirely. It has filled every cell, all available space. There is no room at the inn for anything else. It has me on autopilot, although this is the kind of autopilot that is programmed to make me crash into the sea. Getting through each day feels not like a victory, but a form of survival. Every day is like Groundhog Day, and as I get to the end of one, I just feel anxious about the next one. Christmas comes and goes, but I cannot remember it. I cannot remember the presents I get or the presents I give. I cannot remember the stocking I make for Edie, or the festive costume I apparently dress her in. I must have dressed her in it, because there, on my iCloud, is a picture of it. I cannot remember the food we eat or the programmes we watch or the games we play. All of Christmas 2014 is a blur to me. It's as if my memory banks from the time have been wiped by a virus. It's as if I spent it all in a coma.

All I remember is this. I just want someone to take it away from me, this part of my head. I just want someone to give me a pill to make me go to sleep and when I wake up, for it all to have vanished.

But at some point, you realise that it won't. You realise that you have to fight back. Somehow, somewhere, the real, rational me finds a space in my head and she starts to shout. She starts to shout: 'THIS IS NO LONGER JUST ABOUT YOU, BRYONY. THIS IS ABOUT YOUR DAUGHTER, AND YOUR HUSBAND TOO. IT IS ABOUT YOUR FAMILY.'

Jareth stands there, smirking. 'She's not going to have a family soon, so it doesn't matter. She's going to lose them all, because she's a terrible human being, an evil one.'

'YOU'RE NOT!' shouts the remainder of the real me. 'DON'T LISTEN TO HIM. HE'S NOT REAL. HE'S A MADE-UP CREATION YOU'VE LIVED WITH FOR TOO LONG. HE'S AN IMAGINARY ENEMY YOU NEED TO GROW OUT OF, FOR THE SAKE OF YOUR DAUGHTER AND YOUR HUSBAND WHO LOVE YOU AND WANT YOU TO BE BETTER. PLEASE, BRYONY. FOR THEIR SAKE, PLEASE.'

And for once, I listen to myself. For once, I choose to take my word for things, instead of Jareth the Goblin King's.

I have had OCD for over twenty years, but only now am I actually sitting in a glass box in the office where I work, telling my boss about it. Only now am I admitting to someone publicly, other than Harry or my mother, what is going on in my head. Only now am I calling bullshit on the lies about having flu or a stomach bug or a virus. Only now am I admitting that something is wrong with my brain, and that I need to take time off to sort out my head before I am forced to do so by being sectioned or something similar.

I've been coming into work every day, a rictus grin plastered on my face, because the terror of being alone at home was too much to bear, but it is exhausting, painting the smile onto my face each morning like circus make-up. I may be doing it in an effort to keep up appearances now that I am a mother – it is my daughter who should be crying all the time, not me – but actually, it's making everything worse. It's doing nobody any good – not Edie, not Harry and not myself. I can't continue to put my husband through this experience, which for him must be like being on a broken rollercoaster. And what if, in ten years' time, Edie came to me and said that she had a pain in her head, and I still hadn't made any concerted effort to sort out the pain in mine? How can I be any kind of example to her, how can I look after her when currently, I am barely capable of looking after myself? What if I make her ill, too? What if I pass down my disordered behaviour? I cannot bear to think of her suffering in the same way I have. I cannot stand that this could happen. I will do anything to ensure it doesn't. Absolutely anything at all.

I'm on the bus to a meeting one morning when I am gripped with icy fear and start to cry. I start to cry and I do not stop for the next six or so hours. I am howling and shivering. It's as if my body has had enough. I get off the bus and walk the rest of the way to my appointment, which is, thankfully, with someone I count as a friend as well as a colleague, and she sends me home where I call Harry to tell him how ill I feel, before passing out.

When I wake up it is to the sound of a key in the door. I don't know how many hours have passed, but it feels like I have been asleep for a day. 'I NEED TO

GET EDIE!' I shout before realising that it is my mother, whom Harry has called for help because he is stuck, desperate, in his office.

'I came as quickly as I could,' she says, plonking herself down on the bed next to me and putting her arms around my shoulders. 'You need to get dressed and put some shoes on, darling,' she says, speaking to me very slowly, stroking my cheek. 'I've got us an appointment at a doctor, a sort of posh one, the one my friend Alicia who lives in Chelsea uses, because I couldn't get an appointment at your GP for about three weeks I'm afraid, and when I said it was an emergency they just told me to call 111, which, given how distressed Harry said you were, was not an option.'

Later, I will wonder what happens to all the people who have breakdowns and can't afford to go to posh doctors, the ones who don't have anyone they feel they can call. It is almost beyond comprehension.

But right now, I am out of it. I do as she says, get in her car, mention Edie again and again and am reassured again and again that Harry is going to collect her. We arrive at the posh doctor's, which is on Sloane Street, near a branch of Agent Provocateur and Harvey Nichols, and as I press the gold button on the door, everything begins to feel faintly ridiculous. I feel huge guilt, like an overindulged drama queen who should probably just pull herself the fuck together. I am buzzed through to a waiting room, where men in chinos talk into their iPhones about re-sale values, and it occurs to me that probably none of them are ill and they are just getting yellow fever vaccines before going on safari. (This is not to say that the very posh are immune from mental illness. Far from it. It's just me pointing out how completely strange I felt, sitting in that room with eyes so puffy they could pass for ski jackets.)

Eventually, I am called in to see the doctor, who is a smart man in his sixties with a surgery that looks more like a swish studio apartment. (I'm wondering if there's scope for a book called *Doctor's Surgeries I Have Known*.) Pictures of his beautiful children and grand-children line every shelf. There is a cornice detail on his bookcase.

'So,' says the man, 'for what reason have you come to see Dr Timothy Ogilvie today, then?'

I am momentarily minded to laugh. Did he actually just speak in the third person? Yes, yes he did.

And then I tell him. I tell him everything. About my paranoia that the police are going to take my daughter away, that I have done something terrible to her. He nods along. The very act of unburdening in itself seems to lift me. When I finish, he leans back in his chair and makes his pronouncement.

'I think it's clear that you are a very competent and capable woman and it's important to remember that you will once again be a very competent and capable woman.' I start to cry. 'So what I'm going to do is write you a prescription for a small amount of Diazepam and then I'm going to call up an expert in this field and sort you out with help as soon as it's possible to do so. And by that I mean in the next couple of days. Does that sound good to you?' I nod. I cry. It does.

Diazepam is not a solution, not at all, but it is a bloody good way to get through the day until one comes along. That night I pop a pill and sleep solidly for the first time in months. I am spaced out, slurring my words. I go to work, speak to my boss through blurry tears. There are, I see, tears in her own eyes – tears that tell me she understands all too well what I am experiencing. 'It's important you tell people,' she says. 'If you don't, there's no understanding.' I think perhaps she is talking about the general 'you', rather than me. As I leave the office I hear a young woman talking to a colleague about the lavender martinis she had enjoyed the night before, and I feel completely disjointed. Astonished, even, that it is still possible to live in this world and feel normal.

The next day, I wake up to find a voicemail from a doctor at the Capio Nightingale Hospital, a centre for people with mental-health issues. I can have an appointment the next evening, which can be paid for by BUPA, if I have it. I am dimly aware of being on some sort of system through work, and call to ask if I qualify for cover.

'You can have six sessions this year and then another six during another two years that do not have to be consecutive,' says the person on the phone, who might actually be a robot. Or am I, now, a robot?

'That's wonderful news!' I say, in an attempt to sound human, and I am rewarded with an authorisation code.

So here I am, a reasonably educated woman, only properly getting help for an illness twenty years after I first developed it – and only then through private healthcare I am fortunate enough to have through my job.

For so many reasons, this approach to mental health has to change.

'Are you finding any enjoyment in anything?' asks my new therapist, who has a warm, open face and kind eyes that actually engage with me. I blink at her.

'Enjoyment?' I say, as if unfamiliar with the concept.

'Yes. What do you enjoy?'

'*Game of Thrones?*' I am grasping at straws.

'You probably think that's ridiculous,' she says, 'but it's not. Even little things that make you happy are important, because the more of them you have in life, the better your wellbeing.'

'So I can argue that my favourite box sets are integral to my recovery?' I ask, cracking a smile for what feels like the first time in forever.

'I think the grin on your face gives you the answer to that.' And I actually laugh.

I'm not going to go into details of the therapy sessions I have. Not only would they bore you, but they are mine and my psychologist's, and as much as I need to be able to trust her, she also needs to be able to trust me.

What I do realise is this – finding really good therapy is like trying to find a good boyfriend. Along the way, you're going to encounter some pretty bad ones. It's hard. It really is. And when you do find someone, it's even more difficult. It's not fluffy clouds and kittens and rainbows. You actually have to work at it, like any relationship. So let me tell you about cognitive behavioural therapy, finally, tens of thousands of words after you first encountered it in this book and many years after I first encountered it in my life. It is challenging, *really* challenging. Just taking antidepressants to sort out your mental illness is like choosing to do geography at GCSE. CBT is like choosing history. (Can you guess which subject I picked? Can you, can you?) It is exactly like being back in school again, without the bribes from your parents to do it right, or the friends and lunch breaks to make it all seem vaguely bearable. For me, the only thing that gets me through those first few sessions is the thought that I am helping not just myself, but also Harry and Edie. I'm here as much for them as I am for myself.

The other day I was rewatching *The Empire Strikes Back* – Star Wars being a not-so-small thing that gives me enjoyment – and as Luke Skywalker went through his training with Yoda, it occurred to me that this is exactly what CBT is like. It's like being asked to perform Jedi mind tricks. You're Luke, sitting in a swamp and saying, 'No way can I pull that X-wing fighter out of the murky waters with nothing more than the power of my tiny brain,' and your therapist is Yoda, saying, 'You can, yes,' and, 'You must unlearn what you have learnt.' And you respond, 'It's easy for you to say as a powerful Jedi master, but I'm a complete mess even without knowing that my father is the most evil person in the galaxy and that I have just snogged my sister,' which, thank God, we won't have to go into because CBT does not involve delving into your past.

CBT is hard because it is basically making your brain do the complete opposite of what it has done forever. It's asking you to go cold turkey from all the ludicrous rituals and compulsions you have done for years and years and years. In my case, as someone with OCD, it is not about getting rid of the intrusive thoughts I have, because you will never do that. (If I told you now not ever to think of me naked standing on my head masturbating, the first thing you would do is think of me

naked standing on my head masturbating. So yeah.
Sorry about that.) What CBT does is change the way
you respond to those thoughts. Because they are just
thoughts. They don't necessarily mean anything. You
don't have to offer prayers to the universe to try to
change them, or wash your hands obsessively to make
them go away. When you do these things, you only
make the thoughts more intrusive. You give them
purchase on your already vulnerable brain. Trying to
make yourself feel better only ever makes you feel
worse.

So what you have to do is expose yourself to your
greatest fears. You have to shout out, 'Yes, my family
will die!' and 'Hey, maybe I am a child molester!' You
have to stick your hands down toilets and not wash
them afterwards. You have to stay with your intrusive
thought without doing anything to calm it. As I said,
it's really hard. But fuck, is it worth it.

My therapist tells me that I should be trying to exercise as much as possible. I respond by telling her that
is a really stupid thing to suggest to me. Telling a person
with depression to get up and go for a run is like telling
someone with alcoholism to skip the vodka and have
some water instead. Because when you are in the grips
of depression, you cannot move. You lie there in bed,
pinned to the sheets by some invisible, malignant force,
like one of Darth Vader's henchman who has failed

his master, your room doubling up as your very own Death Star. (I'm sorry for all the *Star Wars* references. Is talking about *Star Wars* all the time an illness, just as being a Jedi is an official religion? If not, it should be.)

You'd like to be elsewhere. You'd rather be outside-than lying in the dark in your own sweat and self-loathing; you want nothing more than to be able to get up and go for a run like a normal person. But you are not feeling normal. You are feeling empty and shell-like yet curiously full of sadness. You are rooted there, not just to the spot but also to that moment in time, and you are not convinced that you will ever be able to leave it. To escape.

I've always found the 'black dog' a curious way to describe depression because dogs are active, dogs are frenetic, dogs are bundles of energy that do not stop. When you are suffering from depression, you have more in common with a sloth. But I have to take my psychologist's word for the healing power of exercise, because she is an expert on these matters and I am not.

So, one Sunday morning, I set my alarm early and resolve to get out of bed. Getting out of bed seems like a tiny thing to someone who has never experienced the paralysing effects of depression, but right now I feel that I'd probably use less effort and energy pulling heavy articulated lorries than I do trying to get up in the morning. This is what happens. One foot edges over the side of the bed. The other eventually follows like the lemming it is. Improbably, impossibly, I am sitting instead of lying flat. I move to stand up. Left foot forward, right foot forward. I somehow find myself heading in the direction of the bathroom, as if wading through treacle. I feel so tired, so full of absolutely nothing at all. Maybe I should take a diazepam and go back to bed. Block out the day. Tell Harry that I have stomach pains, and ask if he can spend the day with Edie at the swings. But I'm in the bathroom now and I'm turning on the taps and removing the musty bed clothes I've worn for God knows how long. I'm stepping into the shower, under its hot, prickly stream, and I'm crying as I try to wash away the misery of the last few days, scrub away the lethargy that seems to cling to my skin like the smell of stale tobacco. Once out of the shower and back in the bedroom I am in the danger zone. I can get dressed and make to leave the house, or I can get back into the mausoleum I have created out of John Lewis bed linen. What's it to be? What's it to be? The choice I make now could be the difference between feeling like a human again or yet another week of nothingness.

So I get up, and I go out, and in doing so, I find I am quite literally moving towards a better place. God, I hate that this book is going to end with me finding contentment through the healing power of therapy and exercise, giving up alcohol for a bit and eating right, but . . . well, it just is. So deal with it. This is not to say I am suddenly a health guru. Far from it. Discovering the power of running is very different from discovering that you are any good at running. I am not and never will be. I have boobs like sandbags that beat me up as I make my way asthmatically around the local park, as if punishing me for daring to think that this was a good idea. All I am doing for that twenty minutes or so is trying to stay alive. The only thing that matters is that I continue to breathe. It clears my mind and a scientist would probably say it produces feel-good endorphins. I am not a scientist, but I do know that after a jog, everything feels a smidgeon more bearable than it did before a jog. Even if I do happen to look like I've been in the glare of a nuclear bomb.

And so, week by week, I start to feel better. I start to write about my illness. I start to share. I get feedback that simultaneously cheers and saddens me, because although it is comforting to know that there are others out there like me, I cannot stand that at any given moment, they could be going through the unique pain only a head can produce. But I start to realise that the head can also give you pleasure. The fog starts to clear. It lifts. I see the vague outline of other people. I hold my daughter close, and my husband too, and finally, I feel I am waking up from the nightmare that first came to me all those years ago when I was twelve.

Epilogue

Hey there. You. Yes, you! Not so fast. I know, I know – you're all ready to close this book after a fuzzy, happy and, if I may say so myself, soppy ending, and get on to something cheerier like, I don't know, *Mein Kampf*, or *The Hunger Games*. But before you do that, I just want you to know that writing this book made me ill. I'm not saying that in an accusatory way, in a bitter 'God, if it wasn't for doing this book, I'd be gamboling through fields like a spring lamb' way. I'm saying it in a sort of 'never forget that mental illness will probably always be there' way, in a 'look after yourself, look out for it, and you will be OK' kind of way.

While writing this book, I wasn't really looking after myself. I'm not sure anyone really looks after themselves while writing a book, which is silly, really, given it is the writer's equivalent of taking part in a marathon. I was drinking five cups of coffee a day, which is obscene, and chugging through fags as if they were chia seeds, which, as we all know, they are not. Now, it's OK to have a little of what you fancy, but while writing this book, I wanted a lot of what I fancied, be it coffee or nicotine or booze and crap food in the evening. And so it was that as soon as I had finished it, I got sick again. Who knew that writing a book about mental illness might make you, um, mentally ill?

Perhaps I was getting into character, but there was Jareth the Goblin King, grabbing on to my head with his icy fingers, trying to dig them in – at least, I hoped it was Jareth. With OCD, there's always that sense that, no matter how many times you've experienced it, no matter how many times you haven't turned out to be a child-molesting maniac, this time could be the exception to the rule.

It was after a New Year's Eve party that I realised Jareth was back. I had, that week, been to the doctor no fewer than three times to ask him if I was having a heart attack (no, I wasn't) and if the headaches I was experiencing might be a brain tumour – no, they probably weren't, but that 'probably' kept on bothering me, with its potential for catastrophe.

Eventually, through thorough researching of brain

tumours with Dr Google, I realised I was being absolutely ridiculous, and resolved to get healthy again. But
then I started to worry about the New Year's Eve party.
Did I cause a fight? Did I cheat on Harry? Did I try
to snog my friend's husband? With each elimination,
something else popped up, until I was left with the
most deranged way to fill the gap in my memory of
that drunken evening – I hurt my daughter. Clearly. I
crawled into her room, and I hurt her.

I know. It's ridiculous, isn't it? But while writing
this book, ridiculous became my norm. For six months,
I'd been reliving my mad past, trying to get it down
on paper, and it was unsurprisingly a bit like trying
to re-open old wounds. Jareth was back, tugging at
my stomach when I woke up, an actual, physical pull
that occurred in the seconds after my eyes opened
and I remembered how much I had lost control at
that party.

There Jareth was, trying to worm his way into every
crease of my brain. Every time I looked at my darling
daughter, he wanted to show me what I stood to lose.
I tried to stop it with logic and reason but you cannot
use logic and reason on Jareth. And I was aware that
the moment I found relief from this worry, he would
only point out a bigger one elsewhere. It's like banging
away at a heavily armoured door that gets more inde-
structible the more you try. To bash through it, to get
to the other side, you have to be more ingenious than

that. You've got to outfox Jareth. You've got to work out how to demand the key from him, or how to make him so meek that he simply lies down and gives it up, willingly.

And the amazing thing is I can recognise that this is Jareth. Or rather, that it is OCD. I can feel it, tap-tap-tapping at my head, asking for permission to come in. This in itself is a breakthrough and I can credit it to all the therapy I have had. When I was seventeen, OCD didn't sit politely on the doorstep of my mind and wait for me to let it in. It found a cracked window and crept in while I wasn't looking, taking up squatter's rights before I had a chance to do anything. Now, with CBT and the right frame of mind, I feel I can close the windows. I feel I can increase the locks on the doors. I have installed a burglar alarm. So my OCD has to work that much harder to get in and cause a full-on breakdown. It has to be cleverer than I am. And this time, I'm not sure it stands a chance. Jareth, I think, has finally crumbled.

I'm out running on Clapham Common, trying to keep my OCD under control. I'm seeing my therapist again. She tells me that Jareth will always be there – it's whether or not I have the strength to put him into hibernation. So running, eating well and watching *Star Wars* and *Game of Thrones*. All of these things are helping me to send Jareth into a coma. I'm OK, I'm OK, I'm OK. I'm going to be, for my husband and my darling daughter.

Today, on this particular run, it is icy cold and the wind is up, making me feel like it will never be spring again. But I've got to get out there. I've got to raise some fucking endorphins.

I decide, that day, not to listen to music but to the radio. I tune in to Radio 4 as I set off, and by chance catch the start of a documentary that Jarvis Cocker has done about the author Carson McCullers, whose first book, *The Heart Is a Lonely Hunter*, was all about the isolation felt by a group of American outcasts. I listen intently, as guests tell Jarvis about how exquisitely and painfully McCullers captured what it is like to be a teenager. I learn that McCullers was a depressive who tried to commit suicide. She was also an alcoholic who died in 1967 at the age of just fifty.

The documentary ends with some archive audio footage of McCullers. 'All people belong to a We except me,' she says, a voice from many decades ago, speaking to me today. I slip in some mud and fall to my knees. And I catch myself speaking out loud, into the wind. 'You were wrong, Carson,' I say. 'You were wrong. You belonged to a We, you really did.' A man in smart lycra running pants looks at me strangely, but I couldn't give a toss. I get up, dust myself down, run home, and resolve to find the We that Carson belonged to.

That afternoon, I post on Twitter for the first time in what feels like months. Twitter, I find, is a dangerous place when you're not feeling yourself, as is all social media – I feel I should be looking up rather than down at my iPhone, trying to get out as much as possible instead of spending too long in imaginary online worlds. (Also, it's bad for my kid to see me on my phone all the time.) But today, I have something to offer. 'What if,' I say, over a series of tweets, 'I set up a kind of group for people with mental-health issues, whereby we meet up once a week or once a fortnight and go for a run and share our stories. We could call it #mentalhealthmates.'

'I think you're high on your run,' says my husband, when he sees these tweets. 'What if loads of nutters turn up?'

'That's the WHOLE POINT, HARRY. I WANT nutters to turn up. The nuttier, the better! I want all of us to come together and prove to the world that actually, it's perfectly normal to be nutty.'

Two weeks later, on Valentine's Day 2016, I am standing outside a café in Hyde Park, waiting for some nutters to turn up to my inaugural Mental Health Mates run. It is freezing cold and I am pretty sure I am going to be stood up and that at most it might be me and two other people. I'm wondering if my madness has tipped into a whole other level where I basically make pleas on Twitter to hang out with strangers, while leaving my husband and child at home on Valentine's Day. But then I tell myself that if one person turns up, on this day that can be cruel for some, then it is worth it. If two people show up, I'm going to do a cartwheel.

So you can imagine my amazement when people start to trickle over to me, asking if this is the (whisper) 'mental-health group'. You can imagine my surprise when almost twenty people turn up, looking sheepish and a bit embarrassed and like they, too, might be doing something completely mad. I shepherd them to a table in the café, take tea orders, then excuse myself for a moment to go to the loo, where I have a little cry as I have a little wee. Then I go back outside and I tell them about wanting to find a We for Carson McCullers. I tell them, these complete strangers, that sometimes I think I am a child molester and a potential serial killer, and not one of them gets up and walks away.

'I have two friends who killed themselves,' says one woman, quietly. 'So I'm here to end the stigma of mental illness.'

'I have panic attacks almost every day,' says someone else.

'Me too,' smiles a man across the table.

'Thank you, thank you,' I say. 'How many of us are on antidepressants?'

Almost everyone in the group puts their hand up. At the table next to us, an elderly couple are beginning to look slightly alarmed.And then we all get up with our teas, and we go for a bracing walk around the Serpentine. A couple of people run together. Others share stories of not being able to work for years, of bad doctors and bad therapists and really, really bad thoughts in their heads. Others don't really say anything. But that's OK. All that matters is that they are there.

Nobody is rocking back and forth. Nobody looks strange. We could be a running club, or an exercise group, for all anyone knows. These are people you could pass on the street without thinking anything other than what nice lipstick they are wearing, or how much you like their trainers. This is because, like most people who suffer from mental illnesses, they are completely normal.

We resolve to make Mental Health Mates a thing, and I get back on the tube with a spring in my step. Changing lines, I run from one platform to another in order to get on a Victoria line train before the doors close. I jump into the carriage and find myself standing next to a big, burly man covered with tattoos. He looks sad. I smile at him, because he looks like he could do with a smile.

'This train's been here for nuff time,' he says to me.

'You mean I didn't need to waste my energy and run?'

He laughs. 'I can't run,' he says. 'Got stabbed in the thigh. Hit a main artery.'

'That's terrible,' I say. 'Did anyone go down for it?'

'Nah, I was concussed. But if I saw him in church, I would say, "It's all right, bruv, I ain't going to press charges," because everyone deserves forgiveness.'

I nod.

'I could do with a run, what with the stuff going on in my head,' he continues. I notice that people are clutching their bags closer to themselves in their seats, but I find myself turning to speak to him face to face.

'Stuff in your head?' I repeat.

'Yeah, like depression stuff.'

He lists all the drugs he is on – serious, serious medication, not just your common or garden antidepressants.

'Mood disorder?' I say.

'Yeah,' he nods. 'Something like that.'

'It's important to talk about these things, though. You're good and brave to talk about them.'

'I ain't brave,' he says. 'I'm a normal bloke. I just think you can't let your demons ruin your day.' He pauses for a moment, reaches to shake my hand. The tube is still in the station. 'Man, I gotta get the bus.

This tube ain't going nowhere.' Then he jumps onto the platform, blows me a kiss, and runs off into the distance. Just another one of the We, I think. The We who are everywhere.

Acknowledgements

Firstly, I want to state that a lot of names in this book have been changed (as have some of the details of their backgrounds and jobs). While I may be fine with blathering my life story all over the shop, I know others aren't, and that is something I respect. Nevertheless, there are many people who I need to name and thank for their support in helping this book to come about. My agent, Janelle Andrew, who has been there from the start, and my editor, Sarah Emsley, for planting the seeds of the book. Emma Tait, for her patience and support. At Headline, Holly Harris, Georgina Moore, Vicky Palmer, Frances Gough and Phoebe Swinburn, for being mad girls in the nicest possible way. All of the above for picking me up and dusting me down when the book writing got a bit much.

I also want to give a huge thanks to everyone at the *Telegraph* who gave me the time and space to write *Mad Girl*, and who also gave me huge support when it felt like the world was falling in on itself: Chris Evans, Jane Bruton, Victoria Harper, Marianne Jones, Kate Bussmann, Vicki Reid, India Sturgis, Harry Wallop, Joe Shute. The readers of the paper, who feel like my second family, my home away from home, and who in writing to me and sharing their stories gave me the motivation for this book.

Laura Wilkins, for doing an early read and being an all-round ace friend.

My mum and dad, sister and brother, for putting up with me and helping me. Sue, Jon, Harriet, Tom, Jemma and all of your extended families for being my family too. Edie, for choosing me. And finally: Harry, for loving me and caring for me without ever once judging me. You are everything.

Further Resources

If you think you need help, the following organisations provide great support for people affected by issues covered in this book:

MIND
www.mind.org.uk
0300 123 3393 (open 9 a.m.- 6 p.m. Monday to Friday except bank holidays)
Or text 86463

Rethink Mental Illness
www.rethink.org.uk
0300 5000 927 (open 9.30 a.m. - 4 p.m. Monday to Friday)

Sane
www.sane.org.uk
0300 304 7000 (open 6 p.m. - 11 p.m. daily)

Samaritans
www.samaritans.org
116 123 (24/7)

OCD Action
www.ocdaction.org.uk
0845 390 6232 (open 9.30 a.m. - 5 p.m. Monday to
Friday)

Beat
www.b-eat.co.uk
Helpline 0345 634 1414 Youthline 0345 634 7650

Refuge
www.refuge.org.uk
0808 2000 247 (24/7)

If you want to come along to a Mental Health Mates
meet-up, search for us on Facebook and join our group
for more information on future get-togethers.